OUR HOLY FAITH

OUR HOLY FAITH

BOOK FIVE

LIGHT OF THE WORLD

TAN Books
Gastonia, North Carolina

Originally published in 1959 as *Our Holy Faith Book V: Living Like Christ, In Christ* by Bruce Publishing Company and reprinted in 1998 by The Neumann Press.

Nihil Obstat:
John A. Schulien, S.T.D.
Censor Librorum
Imprimatur:
W Albert G, Meyer
Archbishop of Milwaukee
July 31, 1959

This TAN Books edition has been re-typeset and enhanced with additional content and revisions, including modernized language and updates to the practices of the Catholic Church. Catechism questions and answers have been replaced with the TAN edition of *The Third Council of Baltimore: Baltimore Catechism 1–4.*

Scripture quotes are adapted from the Douay-Rheims 1899 American Edition.

Content revisions and updates by Elisa Torres
Interior design by Caroline Green and David Ferris
Cover design by www.davidferrisdesign.com

ISBN: 978-1-5051-1924-4

Published in the United States by
TAN Books
PO Box 269
Gastonia, NC 28053
www.TANBooks.com
Printed in the United States of America

Contents

Unit 4: The Seven Sacraments

Unit 5: The Sacramentals and Prayer

Publisher's Note

The original editions of the *Our Holy Faith* series textbooks were published between 1959 and 1964. They were compiled by many different authors over the course of several years. Consequently, the texts varied in their organization from year to year, with similar sections appearing with different names throughout the series and often in varying sequences.

For greater ease of use and consistency, we have reorganized each book so that the Catechism lessons, tests, and other exercises are placed at the end of each relevant chapter or lesson. We have also included answer keys for your convenience in the back of each book.

While the teachings in the original editions remain relevant due to the enduring truths of our Faith, it was necessary to update other aspects in order to more accurately reflect the Church today. These new editions have been revised to incorporate some of the changes to the practices of the Catholic Church.

To the extent possible, we have adapted the text to reflect both the ordinary and extraordinary forms of the Mass and liturgical calendars. In addition to these updates, we have inserted, where relevant to the text, traditional prayers and quotes from the Bible, the Catechism, and the saints.

This new Our Holy Faith series is faithful to the work of the original authors. It honors the fundamental and unchanging truths of the Catholic Church and is heavily influenced by tradition. We believe it is the catechesis you can trust with your children's faith.

UNIT 1 The Chief Truths of Our Faith

CHAPTER 1

The Apostles' Creed

> *In the past years we have studied the doctrines of our holy faith in the Apostles' Creed, and we have learned how we should live with Christ in His Church throughout the liturgical year. Our first unit this year will be a brief review of these teachings. It will help us to understand better the truths which we shall learn in this grade: about the Commandments, the sacraments, the Mass, and prayer.*

LESSON 1

Who God Is, and Why He Made Us

The Bible tells us that God is the creator of our wonderful world and that He has put into it all the things that we need. God is the Supreme Being who made all these things out of nothing. He raised man to share with Him His happiness forever in heaven.

God expects us to work with Him in preparing ourselves for heaven. We must fit ourselves for it by doing what God wants us to do. This means we must learn God's will by studying our religion and listening to sermons and instructions, and then put our religion into daily practice.

We cannot love someone we do not know. As we learn to know persons better, however, we often see faults in their

character. These faults make them less lovable. But God is all perfect and the more we know about God, the more we shall want to live for Him and to serve Him.

Knowing, loving, and serving God in this world is like a three-rung stepladder rising to heaven. Think of how little God asks of us! And for how short a time! Compare this with how much God promises us, and for how long! How good God is to us!

TERMS TO KNOW

- chief
- everlasting
- Apostles
- Creed
- serve
- Supreme Being
- truths

What does *ex nihilo* mean?

This is a Latin expression that means "out of nothing." We say that God created the world *ex nihilo*, meaning He created the world and everything in it out of nothing. We cannot do this. You may knit a garment, bake a cake, or draw a picture, but you needed something—materials or ingredients like cotton, flour, paper, a pencil, etc.—to create these things.

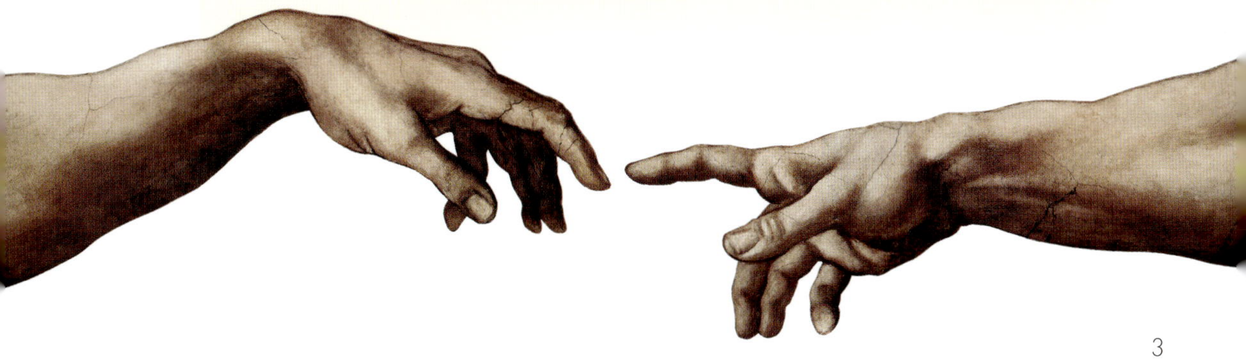

FOR ME TO REVIEW

Catechism Lesson[1]

1. **Q. Who made the world?**
   A. God made the world.

2. **Q. Who is God?**
   A. God is the Creator of heaven and earth, and of all things.

6. **Q. Why did God make you?**
   A. God made me to know Him, to love Him, and to serve Him in this world, and to be happy with Him forever in heaven.

9. **Q. What must we do to save our souls?**
   A. To save our souls we must worship God by faith, hope, and charity; that is, we must believe in Him, hope in Him, and love Him with all our heart.

10. **Q. How shall we know the things which we are to believe?**
    A. We shall know the things which we are to believe from the Catholic Church, through which God speaks to us.

11. **Q. Where shall we find the chief truths which the Church teaches?**
    A. We shall find the chief truths which the Church teaches in the Apostles' Creed.

12. Say the Apostles' Creed.

[1] Question numbers correspond to the questions in the Baltimore Catechism.

FOR ME TO REMEMBER

1. God made all things.
2. God made us to show forth His goodness.
3. God wants us to be happy with Him forever.

FOR ME TO DO

1. Say the Apostles' Creed; Glory be to the Father.
2. Say this prayer together: O my God I want to know You, to love You, and to serve You. I want to do Your will in this life, and be with You forever in heaven.

LESSON 2

How Many of God's Perfections Can You Remember?

Once a king asked a very learned man this question: "What is God?" This wise man named Simon begged the king to allow him one day to think over the question carefully before he gave his answer. The next day he went to the king and begged for two more days. He did the same thing for several days. Finally the king became impatient at the delay. He asked Simon why he postponed his answer so long. The learned man replied, "The longer I consider the question, 'What is God?' the less I seem to know about it."

When our Lord was speaking to the Samaritan woman at Jacob's well, He said, "God is a Spirit." This means He is a living being who can think and will and act, but who has no body.

God told Moses: "I am who am" (Exod. 3:14). No one made God. To which perfection of God does this refer? God is self-existing. There was never a time when He was not. God had no beginning and He will never have an end. God exists of necessity: He is the only One who must be. He always was and He always will be. He could never stop being. We can. We know a little of our past life, a little of what is going on now, but we do not know what will happen in the future. Do we know when we will die? God knows all these things. God knows all things past, present, and future. He knows all things that could have been. He knows not only things that can be seen by everyone but also things that are hidden, even the secrets of our hearts. He reads the thoughts in our minds, hears the words we whisper, and the prayers we say in silence. He sees the things we try to do in secret, when we think no one is around.

God is eternal, omnipresent, omnipotent, and all-knowing.

We should always repeat in time of temptation, *"God sees me and knows all things."*

We can be only in one place at one time. With God it is different. He is present everywhere in all things, at all times. He is on earth, in the sun, moon, and stars. He is in heaven, where the angels and saints see Him. God is all-present.

How wisely God takes care of us! He sees us and watches over us, as a most kind Father. Even if He should let us suffer pain, He does so only to draw good from it.

Think of all the wonderful things God can do and man cannot. Only God can make the sun shine, the rain fall, the grass and flowers grow. Only God could create this wonderful world without any effort. God is almighty. He can do all things.

> *"I believe in God, the Father Almighty, Creator of heaven and earth . . ."*

Understanding the "Eternal Now"

Unlike us, God is outside of time. He lives in the "eternal now," meaning everything is present to Him, or said another way, there is no past or future for Him. It is difficult for us to understand this since we live within time. But some writers and theologians have explained it this way: Imagine your life is a line on a sheet of paper, and you live each day one at a time, moving across the line from left to right. You can only see each day because you are on that line (within time), and you can only move in one direction (you cannot go back in time or skip ahead). But God is the entire sheet of paper; He can see the whole line, your entire life, all at once, and He can do this for everything else in the world as well.

FOR ME TO REVIEW

Catechism Lesson

13. **Q. What is God?**
    A. God is a spirit infinitely perfect.

14. **Q. Had God a beginning?**
    A. God had no beginning; He always was and He always will be.

15. **Q. Where is God?**
    A. God is everywhere.

16. **Q. If God is everywhere, why do we not see Him?**
    A. We do not see God, because He is a pure spirit and cannot be seen with bodily eyes.

17. **Q. Does God see us?**
    A. God sees us and watches over us.

18. **Q. Does God know all things?**
    A. God knows all things, even our most secret thoughts, words, and actions.

19. **Q. Can God do all things?**
    A. God can do all things, and nothing is hard or impossible to Him, because He is Almighty.

20. **Q. Is God just, holy, and merciful?**
    A. God is all just, all holy, all merciful, as He is infinitely perfect.

FOR ME TO REMEMBER

1. God is the Supreme Being, above all creatures.
2. God is eternal, all-knowing, all-present, and almighty.
3. God is our Father.

FOR ME TO DO

1. Thank God often for His loving care of us.
2. Call to mind the presence of God throughout the day to recall that God is present everywhere.
3. Say the Canticle of the Three Young Men (Dan. 3:57–88).

LESSON 3

What Do We Mean by the Blessed Trinity?

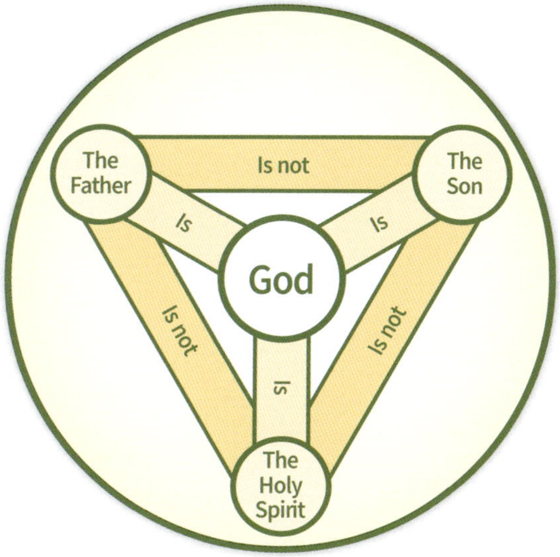

Shield of the Trinity or *Scutum Fidei*, used throughout history to illustrate the Blessed Trinity

From the beginning God taught man that there is but one God. In the Apostles' Creed we say, "I believe in God, the Father almighty, . . . in Jesus Christ, His only Son, our Lord, . . . in the Holy Spirit. . . ." Three Persons, but only one God! This is the mystery of the Blessed Trinity, the greatest mystery of our faith. Each of the three Persons is truly God. They are equal to one another in all things. Each Person is distinct from the others, yet there is but one God! We believe it, because God has told it to us, but we will never fully understand it while we are on earth.

FOR ME TO REVIEW

Catechism Lesson

21. Q. Is there but one God?

A. Yes; there is but one God.

23. Q. How many Persons are there in God?

A. In God there are three Divine Persons, really distinct, and equal in all things—the Father, the Son, and the Holy Spirit.

27. Q. What is the Blessed Trinity?

A. The Blessed Trinity is one God in three Divine Persons.

FOR ME TO REMEMBER

1. In God there are three Divine Persons, God the Father, God the Son, and God the Holy Spirit.
2. The Mystery of the Blessed Trinity is the greatest mystery of our faith.

FOR ME TO DO

1. Make the Sign of the Cross carefully in order to honor the Blessed Trinity.
2. Say the prayer "Glory be to the Father," in praise of the Blessed Trinity.
3. Learn the Sanctus ("Holy, Holy, Holy") of the Mass.

LESSON 4

Who Are the Chief Creatures of God?

Immediately you will say that the chief creatures of God are angels and men. In answer to the question, "What are angels?" you will recall that they are spirits, that is, they have a mind and will but are without bodies. God created the angels to show forth His goodness and to share in His everlasting happiness. But first the angels had to prove their love for God by being faithful to Him. Those who did not remain faithful sinned and were cast into hell. These are called bad angels or devils. The angels who were faithful to God were rewarded and taken into heaven. They are called good angels. These angels praise God in heaven, pray for us, act as messengers from God to us, and serve as our guardian angels.

Fresco from the Mileseva monastery in Serbia, c. 1230 AD, it depicts an angel sitting in front of the tomb of Christ.

St. Michael the Archangel, Pray for Us!

Scripture tells us the archangel Michael was one of the righteous angels who fought in the angelic battle that cast Lucifer and the other unfaithful angels from heaven and into hell (see Revelation 12). Michael's name means "Who is like God?" which is a rebuttal to Lucifer's rebellion. No one is like God, and no one can usurp him, even Lucifer, who was once one of the mightiest and wisest of God's creations. This is why St. Michael is a powerful intercessor as we engage in spiritual warfare with Lucifer and his demons.

FOR ME TO REVIEW

Catechism Lesson

32. **Q. Who created heaven and earth, and all things?**

A. God created heaven and earth, and all things.

"heaven," where God is and will always be. It means, too, everything we see in the sky above us. **"Earth,"** the globe on which we live.

33. **Q. How did God create Heaven and earth?**

A. God created heaven and earth from nothing, by His word only; that is, by a single act of His all-powerful Will.

34. **Q. Which are the chief creatures of God?**

A. The chief creatures of God are angels and men.

35. **Q. What are angels?**

A. Angels are pure spirits without a body, created to adore and enjoy God in heaven.

38. **Q. Did all the angels remain good and happy?**

A. All the angels did not remain good and happy; many of them sinned and were cast into hell; and these are called devils or bad angels.

God did not admit the angels into His presence at once. He placed them for awhile on probation, as He did our first parents.

One of these angels was most beautiful, and was named Lucifer, which means light-bearer. He was so perfect that he seems to have forgotten that he received all his beauty and intelligence from God, and not content with what he had, became sinfully proud and wished to be equal to God Himself. For his sin he and all his followers were driven out of heaven, and God then created hell, in which they were to suffer for all eternity. This same Lucifer is now called Satan, and more commonly the devil, and those who accompanied him in his fall, devils, or fallen angels.

36. Q. Were the angels created for any other purpose?

A. The angels were also created to assist before the throne of God and to minister unto Him; they have often been sent as messengers from God to man; and are also appointed our guardians.

FOR ME TO REMEMBER

1. God, the Creator of heaven and earth, made all things from nothing.
2. Angels and men are the chief creatures of God.
3. The angels who remained faithful are called good angels; they act as messengers from God to us and serve us as our guardian angels.
4. The angels who did not remain faithful are called bad angels or devils. They were cast into hell. They tempt us to do wrong.

FOR ME TO DO

1. Say the Guardian Angel prayer many times each day.
2. When I am tempted I will ask my Guardian Angel for strength to do right.
3. Choose an angel or saint to help me against the devil; e.g., St. Michael, St. Peter.

Prayer to Your Guardian Angel

Angel of God, my guardian dear, to whom God's love commits me here, ever this day, be at my side, to light and guard, rule and guide. Amen.

LESSON 5

Can You Tell the Story of the Creation and Fall of Our First Parents?

Besides the world of angels, God also made the world in which we live. Do you remember the story of how this world was created? On the sixth day God said, "Let us make man to our image and likeness; and let him have dominion over . . . the whole earth" (Gen. 1:26). We recall that the first man created by God was

called Adam, and the first woman, Eve, and that God placed them in the Garden of Paradise.

Just as the angels had to prove their love for God, so did our first parents. How did God test their love for Him? Were they obedient to God? We know that they were not and that God punished them for their sin. They lost sanctifying grace and the right to go to heaven. They lost all the special gifts God had given them, and they were sent out of the Garden of Paradise. As a result of Adam's sin, we have original sin on our souls and, therefore, come into this world without grace. We are happy to remember here, however, that God has helped us by giving us the sacrament of Baptism, as well as the other sacraments and other means of grace.

In Baptism we receive sanctifying grace and are again made children of God and heirs of heaven. But some other effects of original sin remain. We can make mistakes of judgment. Our senses, and imagination, want to have their own way. When we try to pray or study we are distracted. When we try to be good, we have to try hard. It is difficult to control our passions and emotions. Sickness also comes, and at last, death.

The Immaculate Conception

Only one person besides our Lord was ever kept free from original sin. This person was Mary. Mary was so privileged because she was to be the mother of God's Son, and God never allowed original sin to stain her soul. From the first moment of her life, she was absolutely free from original sin. We call this favor her Immaculate Conception.

What is more, Mary herself never committed even the slightest fault. She followed the will of God in all things. We honor her as the most perfect creature. On what day do we celebrate the feast of the Immaculate Conception?

And the Lord God sent him out of the paradise of pleasure, to till the earth from which he was taken.

GENESIS 3:23

FOR ME TO REVIEW

Catechism Lesson

39. **Q. Who were the first man and woman?**
A. The first man and woman were Adam and Eve.

41. **Q. Did God give any command to Adam and Eve?**
A. To try their obedience God commanded Adam and Eve not to eat of a certain fruit which grew in the Garden of Paradise.

43. **Q. Did Adam and Eve remain faithful to God?**
A. Adam and Eve did not remain faithful to God, but broke His commandment by eating the forbidden fruit.

44. **Q. What befell Adam and Eve on account of their sin?**
A. Adam and Eve on account of their sin lost innocence and holiness, and were doomed to sickness and death.

45. **Q. What evil befell us on account of the disobedience of our first parents?**
A. On account of the disobedience of our first parents we all share in their sin and punishment, as we should have shared in their happiness if they had remained faithful.

47. **Q. What is the sin called which we inherit from our first parents?**
A. The sin which we inherit from our first parents is called original sin.

50. **Q. Was anyone ever preserved from original sin?**
A. The Blessed Virgin Mary, through the merits of her divine Son, was preserved free from the guilt of original sin, and this privilege is called her Immaculate Conception.

FOR ME TO REMEMBER

1. Man is a creature composed of body and soul and made to the image and likeness of God.
2. Because Adam and Eve disobeyed God, they lost sanctifying grace and the right to heaven and were sent from the Garden of Paradise.
3. We are born with original sin.
4. The Blessed Virgin Mary is the only person besides Christ free from original sin.
5. This favor is called her Immaculate Conception.
6. Mary was also completely sinless.

FOR ME TO DO

1. Honor the Blessed Virgin by saying: "O Mary, conceived without sin, pray for us who have recourse to thee."
2. Do a kind deed every day to some other person just because he is a child of God like me.
3. Carry a rosary with me. Wear a scapular or scapular medal.
4. Give all my works to Mary, my mother. She will take care of me.

LESSON 6

What Do You Remember About the Sins That Man Commits?

Adam and Eve were not the only ones to commit sin. We too offend God. Our sins are called actual sin. Actual sin is any willful thought, desire, word, action, or omission forbidden by the law of God, for example:

Original Sin	Actual Sin
1. Inherited at birth	1. Mortal or Venial
2. Inherited by all except the Blessed Virgin Mary	2. We commit ourselves
3. Taken away at Baptism	3. Taken away by receiving God's forgiveness, primarily through the sacrament of Reconciliation

1. thought—hating your neighbor;
2. desire—wanting and making up your mind to steal a watch;
3. word—using God's name in vain;
4. action—damaging property;
5. omission—failing, out of self-centered preoccupation, to consider and care for those around me.

There are two kinds of actual sins, mortal and venial. Mortal sin is so called because it takes away the supernatural life of the soul.

Here, let us recall the three things which make a sin mortal:

FIRST: The thought, desire, word, action, or omission must be gravely wrong or be considered a grave matter.

SECOND: The sinner must know or think it is gravely wrong.

THIRD: The sinner must fully consent to it.

When one or more of these three conditions is not fulfilled, there cannot be a mortal sin, but at most a venial sin. Actually it is wrong to offend God even in the slightest matter. There is never an excuse for breaking the law of God in any way. A venial sin is less serious only in comparison with the grievous offense of mortal sin. There is nothing worse in the world than mortal sin, and venial sin is next worse.

FOR ME TO REVIEW

Catechism Lesson

51. **Q. Is original sin the only kind of sin?**
    A. Original sin is not the only kind of sin; there is another kind of sin, which we commit ourselves, called actual sin.

52. **Q. What is actual sin?**
    A. Actual sin is any willful thought, word, deed, or omission contrary to the law of God.

53. **Q. How many kinds of actual sin are there?**
    A. There are two kinds of actual sin—mortal and venial.

54. **Q. What is mortal sin?**
    A. Mortal sin is a grievous offense against the law of God.

55. **Q. Why is this sin called mortal?**
    A. This sin is called mortal because it deprives us of spiritual life, which is sanctifying grace, and brings everlasting death and damnation on the soul.

56. Q. How many things are necessary to make a sin mortal?

A. To make a sin mortal three things are necessary: a grievous matter, sufficient reflection, and full consent of the will.

57. Q. What is venial sin?

A. Venial sin is a slight offense against the law of God in matters of less importance, or in matters of great importance it is an offense committed without sufficient reflection or full consent of the will.

58. Q. Which are the effects of venial sin?

A. The effects of venial sin are the lessening of the love of God in our heart, the making us less worthy of His help, and the weakening of the power to resist mortal sin.

FOR ME TO REMEMBER

1. Actual sins are of two kinds; mortal and venial.
2. A mortal sin is a grievous offense against the law of God.
3. A venial sin is a less serious offense against the law of God.
4. Sin is evil. I must resolve to avoid it.

FOR ME TO DO

1. Pray today for the grace never to offend God by sin.
2. Every night say my Act of Contrition, to tell God I am sorry for all my offenses against His laws.

An Act of Contrition

O my God, I am heartily sorry for having offended Thee, and I detest all my sins, because of Thy just punishments, but most of all because they offend Thee, my God, who art all-good and deserving of all my love. I firmly resolve, with the help of Thy grace, to sin no more and to avoid the near occasions of sin.

LESSON 7

Why Did God Become Man?

The Protoevangelium

After the fall of Adam and Eve, God chastises them for their disobedience, and condemns the serpent. But shortly thereafter, He delivers a message of hope. Genesis 3:15 reads: "I will put enmity between you and the woman, and between your seed and her seed; he shall bruise your head, and you shall bruise his heel." This is the first hint that God will send a redeemer—a Messiah—to save humanity and crush the enemy. This, of course, is Jesus, and the "woman" from this passage refers to Mary. This biblical passage is called the "Protoevangelium." *Proto* means "first," and *evangelium* means "good news" or "gospel." Thus, this is referred to as the "first gospel," the first announcement of the coming of the Messiah.

After the sin of Adam and Eve God did not abandon them, that is, He did not leave them alone, nor did He forget them. God knew that man left to himself could not gain heaven. Therefore, He showed His great mercy by promising to send into the world a redeemer who would free man from his sins and reopen the gates of heaven.

Whom did God send to fulfill this promise? When the Second Person of the Blessed Trinity became man He did not cease to be God, so Jesus Christ was both God and man, true God and true man. Therefore we say, Christ is only one Person, but has two natures, the nature of God and the nature of man. As God, He always was and always will be. As man He had a beginning. We know and love the story of Christmas for on that day, in Bethlehem, more than two millenia ago, Christ was born of the Blessed Virgin Mary.

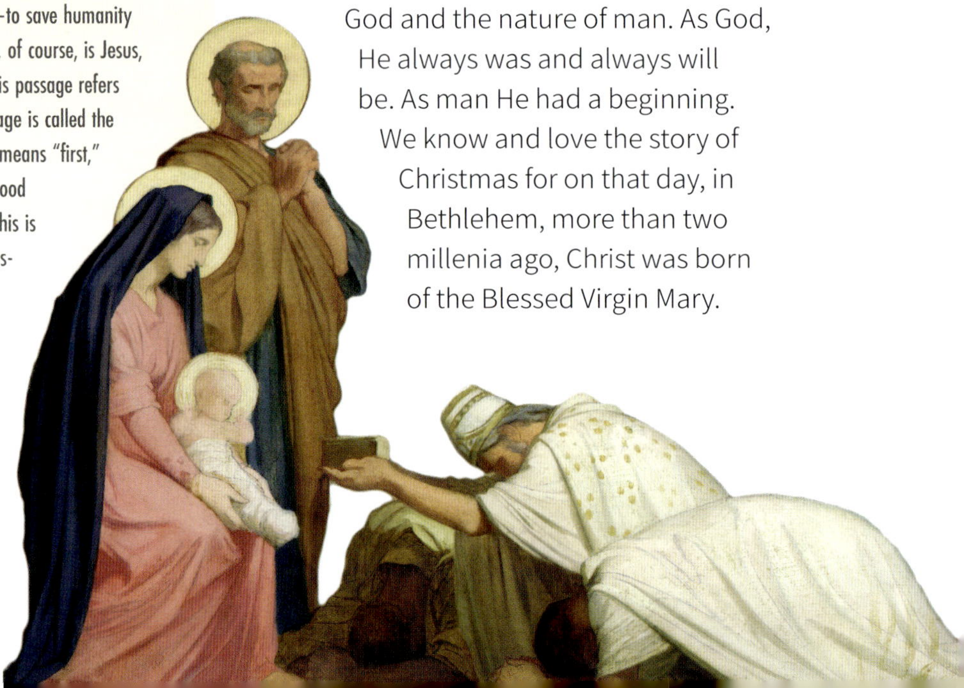

> *"I believe in Jesus Christ, His only Son Our Lord, who was conceived by the Holy Spirit, born of the Virgin Mary . . ."*

FOR ME TO REVIEW

Catechism Lesson

60. **Q. Did God abandon man after he fell into sin?**
A. God did not abandon man after he fell into sin, but promised him a Redeemer, who was to satisfy for man's sin and reopen to him the gates of heaven.

61. **Q. Who is the Redeemer?**
A. Our Blessed Lord and Saviour Jesus Christ is the Redeemer of mankind.

62. **Q. What do you believe of Jesus Christ?**
A. I believe that Jesus Christ is the Son of God, the Second Person of the Blessed Trinity, true God and true man.

66. **Q. Is Jesus Christ more than one person?**
A. No, Jesus Christ is but one Divine Person.

65. **Q. How many natures are there in Jesus Christ?**
A. In Jesus Christ there are two natures, the nature of God and the nature of man.

75. **Q. On what day was Christ born?**
A. Christ was born on Christmas day in a stable at Bethlehem, over nineteen hundred years ago.

FOR ME TO REMEMBER

1. God sent His Son, Jesus Christ, to be our Redeemer and to reopen the gates of heaven.
2. Jesus Christ is the second Person of the Blessed Trinity.
3. Jesus Christ has two natures united in Himself: the nature of God and the nature of man.
4. There are not two persons in Christ, but only one, the Second Person of the Trinity.

FOR ME TO DO

1. Say often during the day, "Blessed be Jesus Christ, true God and true Man."
2. Give thanks to God for having sent Christ to redeem us.
3. Have a crucifix or a shrine in my room to remind me to be grateful to Christ.
4. Develop a deep love of the Sacred Heart of Jesus.

LESSON 8

How Was God as Man Able to Save Us?

Because of His great love for man, Jesus Christ spent thirty-three years in teaching us the way to heaven. He then offered His sufferings and death to God in satisfaction for the sins of men. Christ endured suffering and death to show His great love for us and His strong hatred of sin.

In the Apostles' Creed we say that Christ descended into hell. After He died, the soul of Christ descended into a place or state of rest called limbo, where the souls of the just were waiting for Him. We are not to think of "hell" here as the place where the damned suffer forever. He announced to these souls the joyful tidings of the Redemption. What is meant by the Redemption? Recall the story of the first Easter Sunday.

Christ spent forty days on earth after He arose from the dead. He then ascended into heaven where He sits at the right hand of God the Father Almighty. This means that because Jesus is God, He is equal to the Father and as man He has the highest place in heaven next to God. We also know and believe that this same Christ will come at the end of time on the last day to judge everyone who has ever lived in this world.

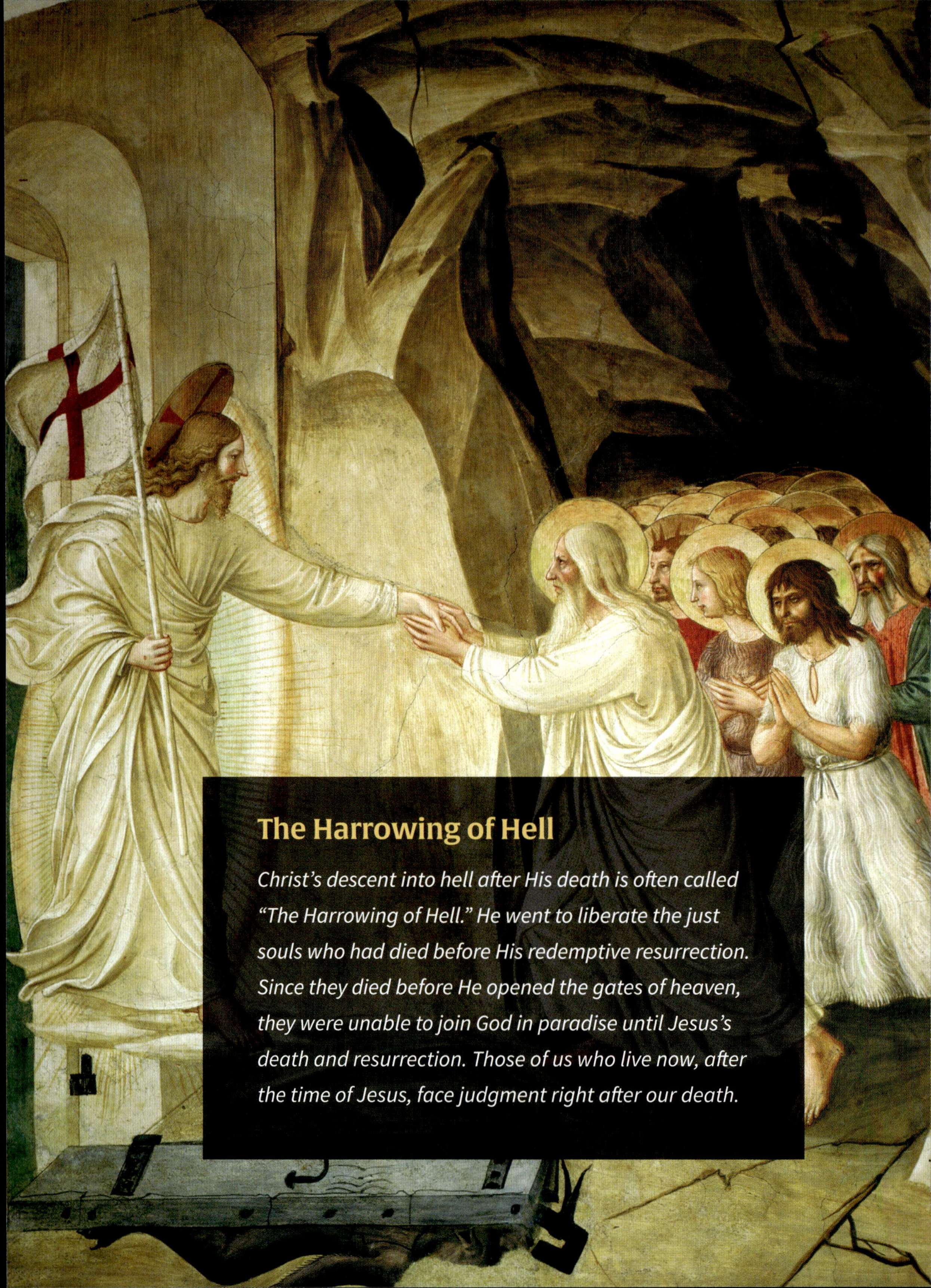

The Harrowing of Hell

Christ's descent into hell after His death is often called "The Harrowing of Hell." He went to liberate the just souls who had died before His redemptive resurrection. Since they died before He opened the gates of heaven, they were unable to join God in paradise until Jesus's death and resurrection. Those of us who live now, after the time of Jesus, face judgment right after our death.

FOR ME TO REVIEW

Catechism Lesson

83. **Q. Why did Christ suffer and die?**
A. It was not necessary for our Lord to suffer so much, but He did it to show how much He loved us and valued our souls, and how much He was willing to give for them.

84. **Q. What lessons do we learn from the sufferings and death of Christ?**
A. From the sufferings and death of Christ we learn the great evil of sin, the hatred God bears to it, and the necessity of satisfying for it.

85. **Q. Whither did Christ's soul go after His death?**
A. After Christ's death, His soul descended into hell.

86. **Q. Did Christ's soul descend into the hell of the damned?**
A. The hell into which Christ's soul descended was not the hell of the damned, but a place or state of rest called limbo, where the souls of the just were waiting for Him.

89. **Q. On what day did Christ rise from the dead?**
A. Christ rose from the dead, glorious and immortal, on Easter Sunday, the third day after His death.

91. **Q. After Christ had remained forty days on earth whither did He go?**
A. After forty days Christ ascended into heaven, and the day on which He ascended into heaven is called Ascension day.

93. **Q. What do you mean by saying that Christ sits at the right hand of God?**
A. When I say that Christ sits at the right hand of God I mean that Christ as God is equal to His Father in all things, and that as man He is in the highest place in heaven next to God.

69. Q. **What do we mean by "Judge the living and the dead"?**

A. By the "living" we mean all those who shall be alive upon the earth at the last day, and by the "dead" those who have died before that time. Or the "living" may also mean those who are in a state of grace; and the "dead" those who are in mortal sin.

FOR ME TO REMEMBER

1. Jesus Christ redeemed us by offering His sufferings and death to God to atone, that is, to make up for our sins.
2. When we say that Christ descended into hell, we mean that He descended into limbo, which is a place or state of rest.
3. Jesus Christ ascended into heaven forty days after Easter.
4. Jesus Christ will judge everyone who has ever lived in this world.
5. As man He sits at the right hand of God.

FOR ME TO DO

1. Look at the crucifix and recite the Act of Contrition.
2. Thank Christ in my own words for suffering and dying for me.
3. Think of some act of self-denial I can perform to show Christ that I appreciate His sufferings and death.
4. Occasionally say the Stations during a visit to Church.
5. Carry something which shows I am a Catholic.

LESSON 9

How Does the Holy Spirit Work in Us?

When we reviewed the lesson on the Blessed Trinity, we said that the Holy Spirit is the Third Person of the Blessed Trinity. The Holy Spirit is often pictured as a dove because this is the form He took when He appeared at the time of Christ's baptism. At another time He came in the form of tongues of fire. Do you remember on what occasion this was? Just as the Holy Spirit came upon the Apostles to sanctify them, so He comes to us to sanctify us through the gift of grace. There are two kinds of grace. Do you know them?

The first is sanctifying grace, given to us in Baptism. It is a sharing in the life of God Himself. It makes us adopted children of God, with the right to heaven. As long as we are free from mortal sin we are said to be living in the state of sanctifying grace. God is in us. We are then temples of the Holy Spirit and we are holy and pleasing to God.

TERMS TO KNOW

- Sanctifying grace
- Actual grace

Actual grace is a special supernatural help from God which helps us to do a thing here and now. It is unlike sanctifying grace in that it is a passing help; it does not remain with us all the time. God gives us actual grace when we need it to help us understand things more clearly or to make our wills strong to do good and to avoid evil. We say that God gives us this grace when we need it. We must, however, pray and ask for this special supernatural help from God. We receive grace through the sacraments, especially the Holy Eucharist. Through this sacrament we receive a special right to actual graces and an increase of sanctifying grace.

FOR ME TO REVIEW

Catechism Lesson

94. Q. Who is the Holy Spirit?

A. The Holy Spirit is the Third Person of the Blessed Trinity.

100. Q. Why did Christ send the Holy Spirit?

A. Christ sent the Holy Spirit to sanctify His Church, to enlighten and strengthen the Apostles, and to enable them to preach the Gospel.

104. Q. How many kinds of grace are there?

A. There are two kinds of grace—sanctifying grace and actual grace.

105. Q. What is sanctifying grace?

A. Sanctifying grace is that grace which makes the soul holy and pleasing to God.

110. Q. What is actual grace?

A. Actual grace is that help of God which enlightens our mind and moves our will to shun evil and do good.

114. Q. Which are the means instituted by our Lord to enable men at all times to share in the fruits of the Redemption?

A. The means instituted by our Lord to enable men at all times to share in the fruits of His Redemption are the Church and the sacraments.

FOR ME TO REMEMBER

1. The Holy Spirit, the Third Person of the Blessed Trinity, makes us holy through the gift of grace.
2. There are two kinds of grace: sanctifying grace and actual grace.
3. We obtain grace through the sacraments and prayer, and especially the Holy Eucharist.
4. We should use every means possible to get actual grace.

A monstrance is used as a receptacle for which the consecrated Host is exposed for veneration.

FOR ME TO DO

1. Make a resolution to use the actual grace which the Holy Spirit gives me.
2. Receive Holy Communion as often as I can.
3. Make acts of spiritual communion (communion of desire).

LESSON 10

In What Special Ways Does the Holy Spirit Help Us?

In Baptism we receive the gift of sanctifying grace and with it certain powers to enable us to perform supernatural acts that can lead us to God. Chief of these powers are the three theological virtues. Among others are the seven gifts of the Holy Spirit. What are these theological virtues? Faith, we remember, is the virtue by which we firmly believe, on the word of God, all the truths He has revealed. Hope, we know, is the virtue by which we trust that God will give us eternal happiness and the means to obtain it. What is charity? It is that virtue by which we love God above all things for His own sake, and our neighbor as ourselves for the love of God.

The seven gifts of the Holy Spirit are:

- wisdom,
- understanding,
- counsel,
- fortitude,
- knowledge,
- piety,
- and fear of the Lord.

In what special way does each of these gifts help us to get to heaven?

FOR ME TO REVIEW

Catechism Lesson

469. Q. What kind of virtues are faith, hope and charity?

A. Faith, hope and charity are called infused theological virtues to distinguish them from the four moral virtues—prudence, justice, fortitude and temperance.

465. Q. What is faith?

A. Faith is a divine virtue by which we firmly believe the truths which God has revealed.

466. Q. What is hope?

A. Hope is a divine virtue by which we firmly trust that God will give us eternal life and the means to obtain it.

467. Q. What is charity?

A. Charity is a divine virtue by which we love God above all things for His own sake, and our neighbor as ourselves for the love of God.

699. Q. Which are the gifts of the Holy Spirit?

A. The gifts of the Holy Spirit are wisdom, understanding, counsel, fortitude, knowledge, piety, and fear of the Lord.

FOR ME TO REMEMBER

1. Faith, hope, and charity are the three theological virtues.
2. Wisdom, understanding, counsel, fortitude, knowledge, piety, and fear of the Lord are the seven gifts of the Holy Spirit.
3. Faith is the virtue by which we believe all the truths revealed by God.
4. Hope is the virtue by which we trust that God will give us eternal happiness and the means to obtain it.
5. Charity is the virtue by which we love God above all things for His own sake, and our neighbor as ourselves for the love of God.
6. By praying the Acts of Faith, Hope, and Charity we can grow closer to God.

FOR ME TO DO

1. Say the Acts of Faith, Hope, and Charity with love and devotion.
2. Learn the prayer of the children of Fatima, beginning with, "My God, I believe, I adore, I hope, and I love Thee…"

The Pardon Prayer of the Children of Fatima

My God, I believe, I adore, I hope and I love Thee! I ask pardon for those who do not believe, do not adore, do not hope and do not love Thee.

LESSON 11

Why Is the Catholic Church a Safe Guide to Heaven?

While Christ was on earth He founded His Church to bring all men to eternal salvation. We must remember that by the word, "Church," we do not mean a building. The Church is a gathering or a congregation of all baptized persons who are united: by believing the same truths which are found in the Apostles' Creed; by offering the same sacrifice which is the holy sacrifice of the Mass, by receiving the same sacraments. In addition, they are governed by the same visible head, our Holy Father, the Pope in Rome.

Christ chose twelve Apostles. Upon them He built His Church. To these men He gave the power to teach and to sanctify (or make holy) the members of His Church. He also gave the Apostles the power to govern His Church. These Apostles have their successors in the Church today. Do you know who they are?

All Christ's Apostles were given these powers; however, Christ gave St. Peter a special power and position. St. Peter became the chief teacher and head of the Apostles. Christ made St. Peter the rock on which the Church was built. He thus became the first

Pope, or ruler of the entire Church. Today, who is the successor of St. Peter?

To help him our Holy Father, the Pope, appoints bishops to act as the head of areas called dioceses. Priests, especially parish priests, help the bishops in the care of souls in the various dioceses.

FOR ME TO REVIEW

Catechism Lesson

115. Q. What is the Church?

A. The Church is the congregation of all those who profess the faith of Christ, partake of the same Sacraments, and are governed by their lawful pastors under one visible head.

120. Q. Why did Christ found the Church?

A. Christ founded the Church to teach, govern, sanctify, and save all men.

117. Q. Who is the visible Head of the Church?

A. Our Holy Father the Pope, the Bishop of Rome, is the Vicar of Christ on earth and the visible Head of the Church.

18. Q. Why is the Pope, the Bishop of Rome, the visible Head of the Church?

A. The Pope, the Bishop of Rome, is the visible Head of the Church because he is the successor of St. Peter, whom Christ made the chief of the Apostles and the visible Head of the Church.

119. Q. Who are the successors of the other Apostles?

A. The successors of the other Apostles are the Bishops of the Holy Catholic Church.

Thou art Peter, and upon this rock I shall build my Church.

MATTHEW 16:18

FOR ME TO REMEMBER

1. Christ founded the Church to bring all men salvation.
2. The Apostles were the first bishops of the Church.
3. Christ made St. Peter the first head of the entire Church.
4. The bishops are successors of the Apostles. Priests are their helpers.

FOR ME TO DO

1. Every day pray for our Holy Father, the Pope, our bishops, and all priests.
2. Help the priests of my parish in every way I can.
3. Show deep respect for God's priests.

LESSON 12

How Can You Recognize the True Church?

The true Church must have certain signs by which it can be recognized. The Catholic Church alone has these signs or marks. It is *one*, which means that the Catholic Church all over the world believes the same truths, receives the same sacraments, has the same sacrifice of the Mass, and is governed by the same head. It is *holy* because its founder, Jesus Christ, is holy, its teachings are holy, it has means to make its members holy, and it helps its members to live holy lives. It is *catholic*, which means that it is intended for everyone for all time, is everywhere, and it teaches all the truths God has revealed. It is *apostolic* because it was founded by Christ on His Apostles whose successors are still governing it.

Now that we have seen that the Catholic Church is the true Church founded by Christ, we can understand that all people are obliged in some way to belong to it in order to be saved.

> *"I believe in the Holy Catholic Church . . ."*

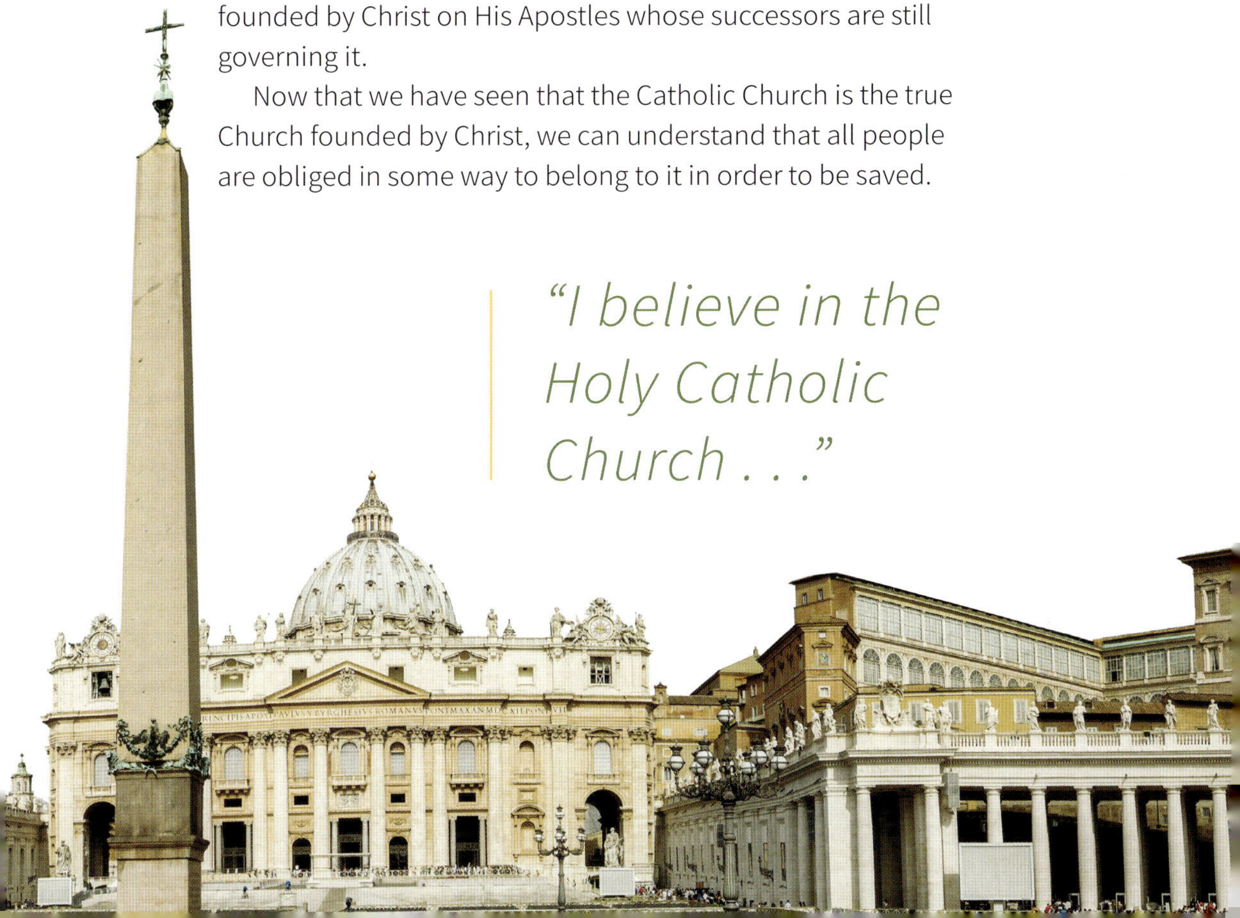

FOR ME TO REVIEW

Catechism Lesson

128. Q. Has the Church any marks by which it may be known?

A. The Church has four marks by which it may be known: it is one; it is holy; it is catholic; it is apostolic.

121. Q. Are all bound to belong to the Church?

A. All are bound to belong to the Church, and he who knows the Church to be the true Church and remains out of it cannot be saved.

FOR ME TO REMEMBER

1. The one true Church established by Christ is the Catholic Church.
2. The chief marks of the Church are these: It is *one, holy, catholic,* and *apostolic.*
3. A person should join the Church if he knows it is the Church Christ founded.

FOR ME TO DO

1. Pray for all missionaries who are trying to spread the true faith.
2. Be a good witness to the Church.
3. Learn my religion so I can explain it to those who do not know about it.

LESSON 13

How Are We United With Christ in the "Communion of Saints"?

The saints in heaven are known as the Church Triumphant.

In the Apostles' Creed we speak of the communion of saints. By it we mean the union of the faithful on earth, the blessed in heaven, and the souls in purgatory, with Christ as their Head. We think of the communion of saints as the people who are united in one great family. Christ is its Head; we are its members.

The Catholic faithful on earth who are striving to know, love, and serve God, belong to the *Church Militant,* Christ's Mystical Body.

The holy souls in purgatory who still have to atone for venial sins or for the punishment due to their forgiven sins, we call the *Church Suffering.*

The blessed in heaven make up the *Church Triumphant.*

All these members of the communion of saints can and do help one another. The faithful on earth pray for the souls in purgatory that they may be relieved of their sufferings. Those on earth pray to the saints in heaven. Both the souls in purgatory and the saints in heaven pray for the faithful on earth. It is encouraging to know that we are not alone. All the members must work together, as directed by Christ, who is the Head.

TERMS TO KNOW

- Church Militant
- Church Suffering
- Church Triumphant

We have learned that sin is an offense against God; therefore, only God can forgive a sin. When Christ was on earth He often forgave people their sins. He is God; therefore, He had the power to absolve them. But the wonderful thing is that Christ gave this power to His Apostles and through them to the priests of the Catholic Church when He said, "Receive the Holy Spirit; whose sins you shall forgive they are forgiven them; and whose sins you shall retain they are retained" (Jn. 20:22–23).

The Church Militant and Triumphant, by Andrea di Bonaiuto, 1365-1367, fresco

"I believe in the communion of saints, the forgiveness of sins"

FOR ME TO REVIEW

Catechism Lesson

338. **Q. What does the communion of saints mean?**
A. The communion of saints means the union which exists between the members of the Church on earth with one another and with the blessed in heaven and with the suffering souls in purgatory.

85. **Q. Through what means may we obtain the "forgiveness of sins"?**
A. We may obtain the "forgiveness of sins" especially through the sacraments of Baptism and Penance and Reconciliation.

733. **Q. How do you know that the priest has the power of absolving from the sins committed after Baptism?**
A. I know that the priest has the power of absolving from the sins committed after Baptism, because Jesus Christ granted that power to the priests of His Church when He said: "Receive the Holy Spirit. Whose sins you shall forgive, they are forgiven them; whose sins you shall retain, they are retained."

FOR ME TO REMEMBER

1. The communion of saints means the union of the faithful on earth, the blessed in heaven, and the souls in purgatory, with Christ as their Head.
2. God has given to the Church, through Jesus Christ, the power to forgive sins.
3. The faithful on earth belong to Christ's Mystical Body.

FOR ME TO DO

1. Pray to the saints in heaven to help us; pray for the souls in purgatory that they may be received into heaven.
2. Go to confession frequently (the Church encourages us to go at least once a month) or immediately if I have committed a grave sin, especially if it is mortal.
3. Ask Mary "Help of Christians" to pray for us.

LESSON 14

Can You Explain This Part of the Creed?

At the end of the world the bodies of all people who have ever lived will rise from their graves. Their souls will be reunited to their bodies never to be separated again. Then, Christ will come with great power and majesty, as He Himself has said, to judge the living and the dead. This judgment is called the general judgment. The good and just people will be taken up to heaven where they will share forever God's glory and happiness. Those who have died with unforgiven mortal sins on their souls will be condemned to hell. There will no longer be a purgatory because there will be no need for it.

Before the general resurrection and judgment, however, there will be a particular judgment for each one of us. It will take place at the time of our death. Immediately after we die, Christ will judge us and decide our reward or punishment, either heaven, purgatory, or hell. We will begin immediately to serve our sentence.

We close the Apostles' Creed with the word "Amen" which means, "So it is," or "I believe it to be so."

> *"I believe in the resurrection of the body, and life everlasting. Amen."*

FOR ME TO REVIEW

Catechism Lesson

86. **Q. What do we mean by the "resurrection of the body"?**
A. By the "resurrection of the body" we mean that the bodies of the dead shall be restored to life, rise again on the last day, and be united to the souls from which they were separated by death.

410. **Q. What is the judgment called which all men have to undergo on the last day?**
A. The judgment which all men have to undergo on the last day is called the general judgment.

409. **Q. What is the judgment called which we have to undergo immediately after death?**
A. The judgment we have to undergo immediately after death is called the particular judgment.

412. **Q. What are the rewards or punishments appointed for men's souls after the particular judgment?**
A. The rewards or punishments appointed for men's souls after the particular judgment are heaven, purgatory, and hell.

25. **Q. What does "Amen" mean?**
A. "Amen" means, "so be it" and expresses a desire that the petition may be granted.

FOR ME TO REMEMBER

1. All men will be judged by God immediately after death and again at the end of the world.
2. The Blessed Virgin Mary was raised from the dead and taken into heaven.

FOR ME TO DO

1. Say the Apostles' Creed thoughtfully and reverently.
2. Have particular devotion to the souls in purgatory. Include them in my daily prayer.
3. Say the Act of Contrition every night so as to be ready to meet God.
4. Pray to Joseph and Mary to help me in my last agony.

The Assumption of the Virgin Mary

The Creed

Write your answers on a separate sheet of paper

PART I Matching

Match each term in Column I with its meaning in Column II

Column I	Column II
A. Apostles' Creed	1. A less serious offense against the law of God
B. Mortal sin	2. Three Divine Persons in one God
C. Angels and men	3. Contains the chief truths taught by the Church
D. Eternal	4. A grievous offense against the law of God
E. Blessed Trinity	5. The chief creatures of God
F. Venial sin	6. Always was and always will be
G. Theological virtues	7. The judgment immediately after death
H. One, holy, catholic, apostolic	8. The chief marks of the Church
I. Particular judgment	9. Faith, hope, and charity
J. Redemption	10. The offering of Christ's sufferings and death to God in satisfaction for the sins of man

PART II Yes or No

Answer the following questions with Yes or No:

1. Does the Holy Spirit sanctify souls through the gift of sanctifying grace?
2. Is hope the virtue by which we firmly believe all the truths revealed by God?

3. At the end of the world will our Lord come to judge everyone who has ever lived on earth?
4. Does sanctifying grace give us a right to heaven?
5. Is the Holy Father the successor of St. Peter?
6. Did Christ make St. John the head of the Apostles?
7. Is wisdom one of the gifts of the Holy Spirit?
8. Does Christ have two natures?
9. Did Christ rise from the dead on the feast of the Ascension?
10. Do the good angels help us by praying for us?

PART III Multiple Choice

Choose the correct answer:

1. When we say that God can do all things we mean that He is:
   A. eternal.
   B. almighty.
   C. all-knowing.

2. The chief truths taught by Jesus Christ through the Catholic Church are found in the:
   A. Act of Love.
   B. Our Father.
   C. Apostles' Creed.

3. A grievous offense against the law of God is called:
   A. mortal sin.
   B. venial sin.
   C. original sin.

4. The offering of Christ's sufferings and death to God to make up for the sins of men is called the:
   A. Resurrection.
   B. Incarnation.
   C. Redemption.

5. The gift of grace is given to us by:
   A. God the Holy Spirit.
   B. the pope.
   C. the bishop.

6. The union of the faithful on earth, the blessed in heaven, and the souls in purgatory with Christ as their head refers to the:
   A. forgiveness of sins.
   B. communion of saints.
   C. resurrection of the body.

7. The judgment which will be passed on each person immediately after death is called the:
   A. general judgment.
   B. immediate judgment.
   C. particular judgment.

8. The first bishops of the Church were the:
   A. Fathers of the Church.
   B. Apostles.
   C. disciples.

9. The virtue by which we firmly trust that God will give us eternal happiness and the means to obtain it is:
   A. faith.
   B. hope.
   C. charity.

10. Christ rose from the dead on:
    A. Good Friday.
    B. Easter Sunday.
    C. Ascension Thursday.

PART IV Matching

Match the beginnings and endings of these sentences:

Beginnings	Endings
1. The words "infinitely perfect" refer to God who is	A. bring all men to salvation.
2. Only God is almighty because	B. assist the bishops in the care of souls.
3. Mortal sin is called mortal	C. immediately after death.
4. After Adam and Eve sinned, God	D. He alone has the power to do all things.
5. By the virtue of faith	E. we believe all the truths God has revealed.
6. Jesus Christ founded the Church to	F. perfect without limit.
7. By the virtue of charity we practice	G. because it takes away the life of the soul.
8. The priests, especially parish priests,	H. love of God, our neighbor, and ourselves.
9. All people are obliged to belong	I. to the Catholic Church in some way, in order to be saved.
10. The particular judgment will take place	J. promised to send a Redeemer to free man from sin and reopen the gates of heaven.

PART V Completion

Complete the following sentences by supplying the missing words:

1. When we say that Christ descended into hell we mean that after He died, the soul of Christ descended into (1).
2. Christ has two natures: the nature of (2) and the nature of (3).
3. The chief marks of the Church are four: (4), (5), (6), and (7).
4. The seven gifts of the Holy Spirit are: (8), (9), (10), (11), (12), (13), and (14).

CHAPTER 2

The First Three Commandments of God—Love of God

One day our Lord was talking to a group of people. A doctor of the law, trying to confuse Him, asked Him which was the greatest commandment of all. Can you imagine how the people listened to hear what Jesus would say to this? Jesus answered by quoting some words from the Old Testament: "Thou shalt love the Lord thy God with thy whole heart, and with thy whole soul, and with thy whole mind, and with thy whole strength. This is the greatest and the first commandment. And the second is like it: Thou shalt love thy neighbor as thyself" (Mt. 22:38–39; cf. Deut. 6:5).

LESSON 15

What Is God's Law of Love?

God gave us a conscience to help us to be happy on earth and to get to heaven. Our conscience, when rightly formed, tells us what is right and what is wrong.

But we do not always follow our conscience. As our own experience shows, we can sin and become wicked. To strengthen the voice of conscience, God has given men a set of laws or rules of conduct. He gave them to Moses on Mt. Sinai, amid thunder, lightning, fire, and smoke. Do you remember the story of how the Israelites received the Ten Commandments? Although some of the

people still refused to do as God commanded, others obeyed Him.

Years later Jesus came into this world to redeem us and to show us how to reach heaven. He showed people how to keep the commandments when He said, “If you love me, keep my commandments” (Jn. 14:15–16). He gave us a law of love to help us to heaven.

These, then, are the two great commandments because they contain the ten given to Moses on Mt. Sinai. The first includes the first three commandments of God. Which are the first three commandments? The second commandment of love includes the remaining seven commandments. Which are the last seven commandments?

Through loving God and loving our neighbor, we will be able to receive the gift of salvation and glorify God in this life and in heaven.

FOR ME TO REVIEW

Catechism Lesson

310. Q. Is it enough to belong to God's Church in order to be saved?

A. It is not enough to belong to the Church in order to be saved, but we must also keep the Commandments of God and of the Church.

311. Q. Which are the commandments that contain the whole law of God?

A. The commandments which contain the whole law of God are these two: 1) Thou shalt love the Lord thy God with thy whole heart, with thy whole soul, with thy whole strength, and with thy whole mind; 2) Thou shalt love thy neighbor as thyself.

101. Q. How do we show that we love God above all things?

A. We show that we love God above all things by keeping His commandments and by never offending Him for any person or thing.

102. Q. What does loving your neighbor as yourself mean?

A. Loving my neighbor as myself does not mean that I must love him as much as myself; but that I must love him with the same kind of love, that is, I must never do to my neighbor what I would not wish my neighbor to do to me; but, on the contrary, do unto others as I would have others do unto me.

313. Q. Which are the Commandments of God?

A. The Commandments of God are these ten:

1. I am the Lord thy God. Thou shalt not have strange gods before Me.
2. Thou shalt not take the name of the Lord thy God in vain.
3. Remember thou keep holy the Sabbath day.
4. Honor thy father and thy mother.
5. Thou shalt not kill.
6. Thou shalt not commit adultery.
7. Thou shalt not steal.
8. Thou shalt not bear false witness against thy neighbor.
9. Thou shalt not covet thy neighbor's wife.
10. Thou shalt not covet thy neighbor's goods.

FOR ME TO REMEMBER

1. I must love God above all things.
2. I must love my neighbor as myself.
3. I must serve God and see Him in all people.

FOR ME TO DO

1. Use the Ten Commandments as a guide when I examine my conscience for confession.
2. Show my love of neighbor at least once every day.
3. Do a good deed at least once a day.

LESSON 16

How Much Do You Remember About the First Commandment?

Let us recall that in studying the Ten Commandments or Laws of God, we learned what God wishes us to do as well as what He forbids us to do. Do you know the first of the Ten Commandments? We are warned in this law not to have strange gods. By it we are commanded to adore the one true God to whom supreme worship is due. How can we, as creatures, give God this worship? We can and do worship Him: by faith, that is, believing in Him; by hope, which means trusting Him; and by love, that is, loving God and our neighbor. We worship God also when we adore Him and pray to Him, especially when we participate in the Holy Sacrifice of the Mass.

We sin against this wonderful gift of faith when we do not believe all the truths that God has revealed to us.

We can sin against hope in two ways. One way is by presumption. This means we are overconfident of our ability and are satisfied with ourselves and our own good work to such an extent that we think we can get to heaven without God. We say, "I can do it all on my own!"

Or we may sin by despair. This means we lose hope or trust in God's mercy and goodness. We say, as it were, "My sins are too great. God will never forgive me. Why ask Him?"

To sin against charity would be to have a hatred of God or our neighbor. What might surprise us is the fact that sloth, which makes us neglect our duty to God, is a sin against charity. Other sins against this virtue are hatred, envy, sadness at another's good fortune, and scandal, that is, bad example.

If we frequently worship God by fervent acts of faith, hope, and charity, God in turn will make these acts easier for us and we ourselves will be more prepared to make them. Thus, these virtues can help us become saints.

The first commandment commands us to adore God alone, but it does not forbid us to honor saints. The saints are God's friends. He is pleased when we honor them and pray to them. They offer their prayers to God for our needs. In honoring them we honor Him for His great goodness to His creatures.

People who do not understand sometimes ask us if we pray to the crucifix or statues that we place in our churches and homes. We know, of course, that we do not pray to statues or other images. We pray to persons, not things. We use crucifixes, statues, and holy pictures to remind us of Christ and the saints, just as we keep pictures of our relatives to remind us of them. These holy objects help us to pray better. They aid us to turn our minds to God. They encourage us to imitate the holiness of the life of Christ and the saints.

Veneration vs. Worship

To explain our relationship with the saints and the Blessed Mother, we should understand the difference between the words "veneration" and "worship." Worship is what we give to God. But veneration means to show reverence for, to honor and respect, and this is what we give to Mary and the saints. We honor and respect them, but we do not worship them, and they do not want our worship! In addition to venerating them and learning from their heroic sanctity, we ask for their intercession before God. Just as we ask our brothers and sisters here on earth to pray for us and our family, so too can we ask the saints in heaven.

FOR ME TO REVIEW

Catechism Lesson

1141. Q. What is the first commandment?

A. The first commandment is: I am the Lord thy God: thou shalt not have strange gods before me.

1142. Q. How may we, in a sense, worship strange gods?

A. We, in a sense, may worship strange gods by giving up the salvation of our souls for wealth, honors, society, worldly pleasures, etc., so that we would offend God, renounce our faith or give up the practice of our religion for their sake.

1143. Q. How does the first commandment help us to keep the great Commandment of the love of God?

A. The first commandment helps us to keep the great Commandment of the love of God because it commands us to adore God alone.

1144. Q. How do we adore God?

A. We adore God by faith, hope, and charity, by prayer and sacrifice.

320. Q. Are sins against faith, hope, and charity also sins against the first commandment?

A. Sins against faith, hope, and charity are also sins against the first commandment.

321. Q. How does a person sin against faith?

A. A person sins against faith, 1) by not trying to know what God has taught; 2) by refusing to believe all that God has taught; 3) by neglecting to profess his belief in what God has taught.

327. Q. Which are the sins against hope?

A. The sins against hope are presumption and despair.

330. Q. How do we sin against the love of God?

A. We sin against the love of God by all sin, but particularly by mortal sin.

331. Q. Does the first commandment forbid the honoring of the saints?

A. The first commandment does not forbid the honoring of the saints, but rather approves of it, because by honoring the saints, who are the chosen friends of God, we honor God Himself.

333. Q. What do we mean by praying to the saints?

A. By praying to the saints we mean the asking of their help and prayers.

344. Q. Why do we pray before the crucifix and the images and relics of the saints?

A. We pray before the crucifix and the images and relics of the saints because they enliven our devotion by exciting pious affections and desires, and by reminding us of Christ and of the saints, that we may imitate their virtues.

FOR ME TO REMEMBER

1. We adore God alone.
2. We honor and respect the saints.

FOR ME TO DO

1. Pray every day for an increase of faith, hope, and charity.
2. Honor and respect relics and images of the saints.
3. Have statues and pictures of the saints in my home.

LESSON 17

How Well Do You Remember What You Studied About the Second Commandment of God?

The second commandment is: "Thou shalt not take the name of the Lord thy God in vain." When we consider the greatness of Him whose name we use, we certainly realize the great reverence that it deserves. "In the name of Jesus let every knee bow, of those that are in heaven, on earth, and under the earth: and let every tongue confess that the Lord Jesus Christ is in the glory of God the Father" (Phil. 2:10–11). Think, too, of the miracles that have been performed through the powerful name of Christ. One day when St. Peter was about to enter the Temple in Jerusalem, a beggar asked him for help. Peter said: "Silver and gold I have none; but what I have, that I give thee. In the name of Jesus Christ of Nazareth, arise and walk" (Acts 3:6). Immediately he was cured.

God also demands that we speak with reverence of the saints and of holy things. Think back to the first commandment. Why does God wish us to show reverence for the saints and holy things? When we use the name of God or of Jesus Christ without proper respect, we offend God by taking His name in vain. We offend God further by cursing. Cursing, you remember, is asking God to cause an evil to fall upon a person, place, or thing to satisfy our evil desires, and actually to wish evil to happen.

> *"Blessed be the name of Jesus."*

FOR ME TO REVIEW

Catechism Lesson

345. Q. What is the second commandment?

A. The second commandment is: "Thou shalt not take the name of the Lord thy God in vain."

346. Q. What are we commanded by the second commandment?

A. We are commanded by the second commandment to speak with reverence of God and of the saints, and of all holy things, and to keep our lawful oaths and vows.

1218. Q. What do you mean by taking God's name in vain?

A. By taking God's name in vain I mean taking it without reverence, as in cursing or using in a light and careless manner, as in exclamation.

352. Q. What is forbidden by the second commandment?

A. The second commandment forbids all false, rash, unjust, and unnecessary oaths, blasphemy, cursing, and profane words.

FOR ME TO REMEMBER

1. We reverence God's name by never using it in vain.
2. Good Catholics always show reverence for holy persons, places, and things.

FOR ME TO DO

1. Praise God's name when I hear it used in vain.
2. Say often during the day, "Blessed be the name of Jesus."
3. Bow my head at the name of Jesus whenever and wherever I hear it.

LESSON 18

What Can You Say About the Third Commandment?

You already know that the third commandment is: "Remember thou keep holy the Lord's day." Which is the Lord's day? How do we keep it holy? In answer to these questions we recall that God commands us to worship God on Sunday, the Lord's day. The Church tells us to keep it holy by assisting at the Holy Sacrifice of the Mass. Can you mention other ways by which you can keep the Lord's day holy?

After God had completed the work of creation, the Bible tells us that He rested. Following His example, we are commanded to avoid all unnecessary work of body or mind and rest on the Lord's day. This includes such work as painting the garage, washing or ironing clothes, shopping, cutting the grass, or washing the car. We should avoid work which distracts us from true spiritual leisure and rest. Can you think of other kinds of work? Are any of these ever permitted on Sundays and holy days of obligation? Discuss these with the members of your class or family.

Keep Sundays holy by assisting at the Holy Sacrifice of the Mass

FOR ME TO REVIEW

Catechism Lesson

1242. Q. What is the third commandment?

A. The third commandment is: Remember thou keep holy the Sabbath day.

1243. Q. What are we commanded by the third commandment?

A. By the third commandment we are commanded to keep holy the Lord's day and the holy days of obligation, on which we are to give our time to the service and worship of God.

1245. Q. How are we to worship God on Sundays and holy days of obligation?

A. We are to worship God on Sundays and holy days of obligation by hearing Mass, by prayer, and by other good works.

1252. Q. What is forbidden by the third commandment?

A. The third commandment forbids all unnecessary work and whatever else may hinder the due observance of the Lord's day.

FOR ME TO REMEMBER

1. We must be fully present at Mass on Sundays.
2. We must not do any unnecessary work on Sundays.

FOR ME TO DO

1. Try to be fully present at Mass on Sundays with greater devotion.
2. Pray for the grace never to miss Mass on Sunday through my own fault.
3. Hear an extra Mass for those who do not go.

The First Three Commandments

Write your answers on a separate sheet of paper

PART I Matching

Match the beginnings and endings of these sentences:

Column I	Column II
A. Cursing	1. Remember thou keep holy the Lord's Day.
B. Sunday	2. Calling down evil on a person, place, or thing
C. First Commandment	3. The Lord's day
D. Work to avoid on Sundays	4. Statues or pictures
E. Revealed	5. Great respect
F. Sloth	6. Thinking we can get to heaven without earning it
G. Images	7. I am the Lord thy God; thou shalt not have strange gods before Me.
H. Presumption	8. Belief in God and His truths
I. Reverence	9. Thou shalt not take the name of the Lord thy God in vain.
J. Third Commandment	10. Firm trust
K. Charity	11. Made known by God to man
L. Second Commandment	12. Laziness
M. Hope	13. Labor inhibiting rest and leisure.
N. Faith	14. Loss of hope in God's mercy
O. Despair	15. Love

PART II Multiple Choice.

Choose the correct answer:

1. The second commandment tells us to:
   A. honor God's name.
   B. go to Mass on Sunday.
   C. speak the truth always.

2. We are keeping the third commandment if we:
   A. be fully present at Mass on Sunday.
   B. try to obey our parents.
   C. speak the truth always.

3. When we think that God will take us to heaven even if we do not use the means He has given us to save our souls, we sin against:
   A. faith.
   B. hope.
   C. charity.

4. To curse means to:
   A. swear.
   B. wish evil to someone.
   C. speak an untruth.

5. We practice the virtue of hope when we:
   A. trust God.
   B. show respect for priests.
   C. love our parents.

6. By the first commandment we are taught to:
   A. go to confession often.
   B. worship God alone.
   C. respect the property of others.

8. Work that we should avoid on Sundays requires:
   A. labor that inhibits rest and leisure.
   B. labor of body.
   C. use of machinery.

9. Images of Christ and of the saints are used in our churches because they:
   A. are blessed.
   B. help us to pray.
   C. are decorations.

10. When we speak with reverence of the saints we practice the:
   A. first commandment.
   B. second commandment.
   C. third commandment.

UNIT 2 The Last Seven Commandments of God, Love of Neighbor

CHAPTER 3
Honor Thy Father and Thy Mother

"Thou shalt love the Lord thy God with thy whole heart, and with thy whole soul, and with thy whole strength, and with thy whole mind" (Lk. 10:27). This is the first commandment. And the second is like it: "Thou shalt love thy neighbor as thyself." These are the words of Holy Scripture which tell us to love God and our neighbor as ourselves.

We have learned that the first three commandments teach us how to love God. The other seven commandments tell us how God wishes us to love our neighbor and ourselves

LESSON 19

The Fourth Commandment

"Ah, gee! All that I ever do is wash dishes." That was what Tommy was thinking when he heard his mother's voice coming from the kitchen. Why of all times did he have to work now? Dishes could wait, but his favorite TV show was just getting to the most exciting part.

Yes, Tommy was having a hard time. He was supposed to do what his mother wanted when he would rather watch television. Here, however, was his chance of putting into practice the fourth commandment.

Everyone knows the fourth commandment of God is, *Honor thy father and thy mother.* But does everyone realize what it means? God tells us to honor our parents. By the word parents God did not mean only our mother and father. He meant all those who have authority over us.

God does not speak to us directly. He gives others the right to speak for Him. Those other people can be our parents, the pope, bishops,

TERMS TO KNOW

- lawful superiors
- reverence
- respect
- well-being
- unkindness
- authority

priests, teachers, and officials of our government. They have authority from God. We call them our lawful superiors. In honoring them, we are honoring God.

Just what does the fourth commandment command us to do? By the fourth commandment we are *commanded to respect and love our parents, to obey them in all that is not sinful, and to help them when they are in need.*

Our Lord Himself has shown us how to obey. We have learned that when Jesus was twelve years old, He went with Mary and Joseph to the temple at Jerusalem for the feast of the Passover. When the feast was over, Mary and Joseph started home. Can you tell the story of how they discovered that Jesus had been lost? You remember that on the third day of anxious searching, they found Him in the temple, listening to the doctors of the law and asking them questions.

Then Jesus went back with Mary and Joseph to Nazareth, and as the Gospel says, He "was subject to them." This means that He obeyed His mother and foster father in all things, especially the little things that make up everyday life.

We Must Respect Our Parents

Since our parents take the place of God on earth we must show them respect. We know how hard it is sometimes to take the blame for something we did not do. Perhaps your little brother or sister broke your mother's beautiful vase. Mother didn't blame them though. She blamed you. What can you do about it? If you replied courteously, explaining calmly what happened, you would be giving Mother the respect she deserved.

Respect for our parents and for those in authority is something we often forget. Too often we answer back, shout, or laugh at the mistakes of our parents. Remember, they take God's place. All parents are chosen by God to care for us, body and soul. They deserve our respect. Without them, we could not have come into the world.

Respect demands that we never be ashamed of our parents for what they say or do. Whether they are rich or poor, young or old, educated or not, they are our parents. Even parents who are not as good as they should be must be respected. We owe our mothers and fathers respect always. This deep respect must be in our hearts. We must also show it in deed and in word. Christ gave us a wonderful example of how to act toward our parents. Pray to be like Him at all times.

The lives of the saints and of noble people show us how they honored their parents. Some of them showed great respect for their parents even when they became famous and occupied high positions, for instance, St. Thomas More. Even when he was Lord Chancellor of England, Thomas More kept up his childhood custom of kneeling to ask his father's blessing, often doing it in public.

Pope St. Pius X showed great happiness when he noticed his plainly dressed mother one day in the audience, among the peasants of Italy.

Abraham Lincoln often said while he was president, "All that I am, and all that I ever hope to be, I owe to my darling mother."

At the age of sixteen, George Washington wanted to join his brothers in the British Navy. His mother asked him to remain in Virginia and continue his education. He did. Years later, he became the "Father of His Country."

We Must Love Our Parents

Our Lord loved His Mother Mary and St. Joseph. He always did what they wanted. Do you remember what Christ did for Mary at the marriage feast at Cana? He changed the water into wine at His mother's wish. His love for her was so great that He could not refuse what she asked. Our parents ask us to do many things. If we love them our actions will show it. We will obey them, help them, and pray for them.

Our love for our parents will grow if we stop to think now and then of how much they have done for us.

Once a boy named Thomas sat watching his father make out the end-of-the-month statements to those who owed money for purchases made at his store. Thomas thought this was a very good way to earn money. He decided that he would send a statement to his mother for errands he had run and tasks he had performed. This is what he wrote:

To Mother: For doing the dishes, 3 dollars; for mowing the lawn, 5 dollars; for cleaning the basement, 5 dollars; for taking care of Baby Anne, 2 dollars; total: $15.

In the morning, there at his place at the table was the envelope he was eagerly awaiting. He tore it open. There was no money, only a note. He began to read it. This is what he read:

To Thomas: For taking care of you since you were a baby, nothing; for washing and ironing your clothes every week, nothing; for preparing your meals every day, nothing; for taking care of you when you are sick, nothing; for all the things Mother does, nothing. She did it for you because she loves you and God.

Love, Mother.

Don't we often act as Thomas did? If we truly wish to imitate our Lord, we will gladly help and serve others every day.

We Must Obey Our Parents

We remember that Jesus is God. He knows all things and is all wise. He knew more than St. Joseph or the Blessed Virgin Mary. Yet Jesus Christ, God the Son, obeyed Joseph and Mary. He did not actually have to obey, because as God He was their Lord and Master. Suppose that Jesus was helping St. Joseph make a stool. Jesus knew far more about making it than St. Joseph did. Yet Jesus obeyed His foster father and made the stool just as He was told to, not only because He was asked but because it was His heavenly Father's will. Jesus worked for those whom God had placed over Him promptly, willingly, and cheerfully. He knew it was what God wanted Him to do and He did it. Do you know another reason why Jesus obeyed? He loved Mary and

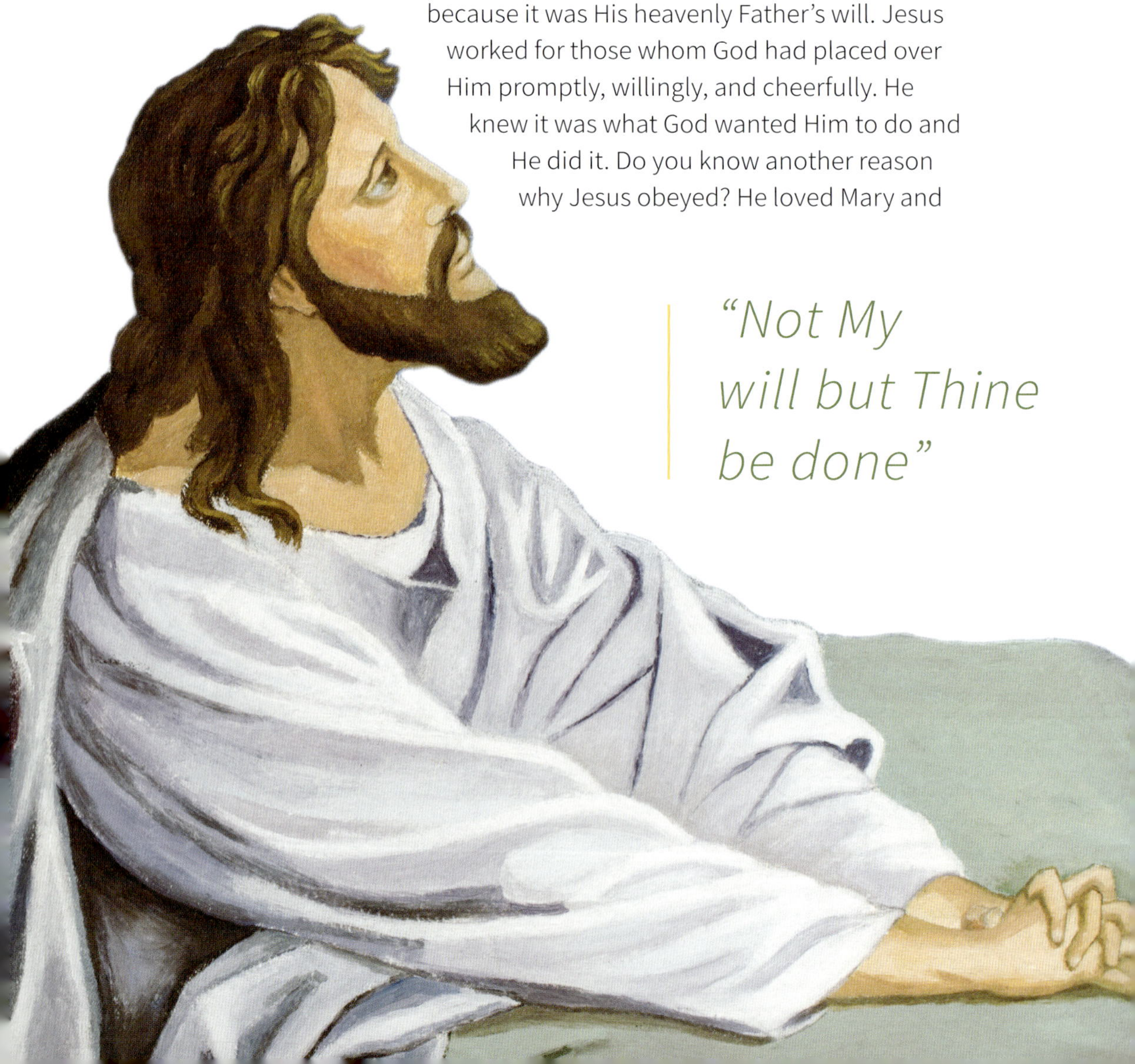

"Not My will but Thine be done"

Joseph. He knew how many things they had done for Him. He recalled Bethlehem, His stay in Egypt, His return home.

Fathers and mothers are wiser than their children. They know more about right and wrong than we do. If we always obey them, we will form the habit of doing the right thing. We should be willing to do not only the work assigned to us but also any other thing around the house that we know needs to be done. If we wish to be truly obedient and to imitate Christ, we will gladly volunteer to do some of these extra duties.

"Not My will but Thine be done" (Lk. 22:43). How familiar those words sound! They are the words spoken by Christ during His agony in the garden. Christ didn't want to suffer but He did. He was obedient even to His death on the cross. Suppose we make His words our own. How? By doing just what we are told to do. When mother or father asks you to do something you don't especially like to do, don't complain. Think of Christ dying on the cross. No complaint crossed His lips. Obedience was the example He gave. Will it be yours?

God commands us to obey in all that is not sinful. If at some time we are told to do something sinful, we must not do it. Obedience to God comes first.

We Must Help Our Parents

From the time we were born, we have received our parents' love. We can never fully repay them for their love, but there are many things that we can do for our mothers and fathers to show them we love them.

Mother and father are busy all day—cleaning, cooking, working. When we finish our schoolwork, the first thing we want to do is play. Of course, we should play, too. However, couldn't we give a half hour or forty-five minutes to help mother by watching the baby, doing some dusting, straightening up our room? Father would be grateful to us too if we took time to mow the lawn, shovel the walk or the driveway, clean the basement, or put the toolbox in order. You suggest some other things you could do for your mother or father.

We also have duties toward our parents when they reach the age at which they are unable to do things for themselves. Think, for instance, how important it is for a son or daughter to help an aged parent who is unable to get out to do shopping, or is unable to do cleaning or things of that kind. It is the duty of children to take care of their parents when they are in need.

We have the responsibility of caring for our parents' spiritual well-being also. If our parents cannot get to church for Mass by themselves, we must help them, if we can. If they are unable to go to church to receive the sacraments, we must notify the priest and ask him to come to their home. Our parents were responsible for our spiritual well-being when we were children. We, in turn, are obliged to take care of them in their old age.

We Must Obey Our Lawful Superiors

One day the leader of the Jews sent the Pharisees and Herodians to Jesus to ask Him if it was right to pay taxes to the Romans. They ruled Palestine at the time. The Pharisees did not want to pay the taxes. The Herodians liked the Romans and were willing to pay the tax money. Jesus asked for a coin. He asked the people whose image and name were on the coin. The people answered, "Caesar's." Jesus told them to give to God what belonged to God, and to Caesar what belonged to Caesar. Jesus taught the people that they owed obedience to those in authority over them in the Church as well as those in the civil government.

The pope, bishops, and priests are Christ's representatives in the Church. Christ appointed them, "to go forth and teach all nations." He made them responsible for our spiritual welfare. These helpers of Christ love us and want to help us. We are obliged to honor and obey them. When and how do we do this? We must try to help them and speak about them with reverence and respect.

Our teachers are also our lawful superiors. They take the place of our

"The obedience which we render to a superior is paid to God, Who says, 'He that hears you hears Me;' so that whatever he who holds the place of God commands, supposing it is not evidently contrary to God's law, is to be received by us as if it came from God Himself; for it is the same thing to know His Will, either from His Own, from an Angel's, or from a man's mouth."

—Saint Bernard of Clairvaux

The Story of Absalom

The story of Absalom, the son of King David, illustrates how severely God punishes disobedience to lawful superiors. We know that King David loved Absalom more than anything else in the world. The boy, however, did not love his father and plotted against him. Instead of honoring his father, he dishonored him by saying that he was not attending to the business of the kingdom. Two armies were formed and a revolt took place. When the armies met, God gave victory to David. As Absalom was running away, his long hair caught in the branches of a tree and he was killed. By his revolt against his father, Absalom brought sorrow to his father and the punishment of God upon himself.

parents when we are in school. They help us to know, love, and serve God. We must co-operate with our teachers and obey them.

We must honor and obey the President of the United States, the governor of our state, the mayor of our city, and all officials under them. These officials of the law have been placed over us by God to keep law and order so that we may live in peace. As children we should form the habit of obeying the wishes of all who are appointed to guide and protect us. Can you name the many persons who would be included in the group referred to in the preceding sentence?

The fourth commandment forbids disrespect, unkindness, and disobedience to our parents and lawful superiors. All authority comes from God. Any person who has received authority to act as a lawful superior represents God Himself. We sin against the fourth commandment if we show disrespect, unkindness, or disobedience to one who has been appointed to direct and guide us.

Sometimes boys and girls dare us to do wrong. They taunt us. They say we are afraid. They try in every way to lead us to do things we know are sinful. We must never follow such leaders. We show that we have courage when we resist their evil influence and obey God.

FOR ME TO STUDY

Catechism Lesson

361. Q. What is the fourth commandment?

A. The fourth commandment is: "Honor thy father and thy mother."

362. Q. What are we commanded by the fourth commandment?

A. We are commanded by the fourth commandment to honor, love, and obey our parents in all that is not sin.

365. Q. What is forbidden by the fourth commandment?

A. The fourth commandment forbids all disobedience, contempt, and stubbornness towards our parents or lawful superiors.

- *Why must we obey our parents?*
- *How can we show respect for our parents?*
- *When is the only time we are not obliged to obey our parents?*
- *Who are our lawful superiors?*
- *How can we show reverence for the President of the United*

States? our state governor? our mayor?

- *Are you imitating our Lord if you do for your parents only the things they command you to do?*
- *In what ways can you show your respect and obedience to the priests of the parish? to your teacher?*
- *How will obedience to your parents help to make your home happy?*

FOR ME TO REMEMBER

1. All authority comes from God.
2. In the fourth commandment God tells us to love, honor, and obey our parents and lawful superiors.
3. God has forbidden us to disobey our parents or to show them any unkindness or disrespect.
4. We please God by our obedience and draw down His blessings upon us.

FOR ME TO DO

1. Each day I will say my Act of Faith, Hope, and Love to renew my obedience to Christ and to the Church.
2. I will volunteer to help at home tonight without waiting to be asked.
3. I will do my work in school this morning as well as I can.

4. I will learn the traffic rules for riding a bicycle and follow them carefully.
5. At Mass I will ask our Lord to bless my home, my father, mother, brothers, and sisters.

CHAPTER 4

Thou Shalt Not Kill

LESSON 20

The Fifth Commandment

Life is a divine gift. It is not like a human gift. When someone we love gives us a gift, we receive it with pleasure and use it carefully. But once the gift is given to us, it becomes our own to use as we wish. The one who gave it to us does not expect us to return it. The gift of life, however, when given to men by God, never becomes theirs to use as they please. They must use this gift in the way God wishes them to. They must also respect this gift of God to others.

When God gave Moses the Ten Commandments He said very clearly: Thou shalt not kill! This law, which God had put in man's heart when He created him, and then gave to Moses on the tablet of stone, is the fifth commandment.

Do you know what we are commanded by the fifth commandment? By the fifth commandment we are commanded to take proper care of our own spiritual and bodily well-being and that of our neighbor.

Our Spiritual Well-Being

God made us creatures composed of body and soul. He created us to know, love, and serve Him on earth and to be happy with Him forever in eternity. God wants us to enjoy His gifts so much that He gave us a special command telling us to take care of our body and our soul. The care we take of our soul protects our spiritual welfare. The care we take of our body protects our bodily welfare.

Is it important that we use these means of grace? It is just as important to make frequent use of these gifts by which we take proper care of our spiritual well-being as it is to use all the helps we have to take the proper care of our bodily well-being. We know what would happen to our bodies if we neglected to follow reasonable rules about eating, sleeping, playing, and the like. Our spiritual life, too, would be weakened if we did not make use of all the helps God has given us for our spiritual well-being.

Sources of Grace

The supernatural life of our soul is strengthened by grace. How do we get grace? To answer this question you need only think of the many ways you yourself have obtained grace. The prayers you say devoutly are a source of grace. What prayers have you said already today? You were present at Mass on Sunday. Perhaps you went to Mass this morning. This was another source of grace. If you received our Lord in Holy Communion, you made use of another main source of grace. When you go to Confession you gain grace in another way. These are all ways by which you can take proper care of your spiritual well-being.

Our Bodily Well-Being

The fifth commandment also commands us to take care of our bodily well-being. We do this by following rules of health and safety. You know many ways by which you can help your body grow strong and healthy. Mention some of them now. The rules of safety, too, are necessary for the well-being of our bodies. You might discuss these rules.

When we studied the fourth commandment, we learned that we must obey and respect the laws of our city or state. By our obedience to health and safety rules at home, at school, and at play, we also obey God's fifth commandment: Thou shalt not kill.

Our Neighbors' Spiritual Well-Being

We can take care of our neighbors' spiritual well-being in several ways. We can pray for others and make sacrifices to obtain God's help for them. We can help them by giving a good example. We can help them to fulfill their religious duties. Every good thing we do may help some person to know, love, and serve God better.

Our Neighbor's Bodily Well-Being

Do you know the story of the good Samaritan? What did he do for his neighbor? Was the poor man who was beaten by the robbers a friend of his?

Our Lord has promised that everything we do for our neighbor will be rewarded as though we had done it for Him. This should help us to be kind, helpful, and polite to all of God's children.

Do you know the story of St. Martin of Tours? A poor shivering man begged him for money. He had no money, but to show his sympathy he took his sword and cut his beautiful military cloak in two. Then he covered the poor beggar with half of the cloak and

The good Samaritan helped an injured stranger.

continued his journey. That night, as Martin slept, a Visitor came to him. It was Christ Himself, wearing half of Martin's cloak.

To help us understand more fully what is meant by taking proper care of our own and our neighbor's spiritual and bodily well-being, let us examine what is forbidden by the fifth commandment. Briefly it is this: *The fifth commandment forbids murder and suicide, and also fighting, inordinate anger, hatred, revenge, drunkenness, and bad example.* Let us look at each of these.

Willful Murder. Willful murder means unjustly taking the life of another person. Murder is a grievous sin. It interferes with the rights of God as the Lord of life and death and the right of man to self-preservation. When Cain murdered his brother, he destroyed what belonged both to God and man. God said to Cain: "And now cursed are you on the soil which has opened its mouth to receive your brother's blood from your hand" (Gen. 4:11). This was the first murder. God punished it severely.

The fifth commandment also forbids us to do anything that could cause bodily harm to ourselves or others. Sometimes we injure others through our thoughtlessness. A boy throws stones and because of his carelessness his friend loses an eye. A driver speeds in his car. Or this, for instance: Herbert pours water on his sidewalk one very cold day so he can have an icy slide. An old man comes along and slips and breaks his leg. Is Herbert

The first act of murder was punished severely by God.

remembering the fifth commandment? Sometimes children play ball on busy streets or risk their lives in heavy traffic, for example, on bicycles. Are we pleasing God when we take chances with our own lives or the lives of other people?

Suicide. May we ever take our own life? Never. Suicide is a serious sin. God is always watching over us and taking care of us. A person who deliberately takes his own life acts as if it was he, not God, who owned life. He treats life as if it belonged to him, not to God. Since life belongs to God, only God can end the life which He has given.

Sometimes people commit suicide when they are out of their minds, and do not really know what they are doing. Is this a mortal sin? why not? What are the three things necessary to make a sin mortal?

Father William Doyle was an Army chaplain. One night he crawled from foxhole to foxhole to give the Last Sacraments to dying soldiers. He was struck by a bomb and killed. Did he commit suicide? There are times when we may risk our life to save another. We may, for example, leap into the ocean to save someone who is in danger of drowning, even though the waves are so high that we ourselves may easily drown in our attempt to save him. Doctors and nurses risk their lives on battlefields, or when they take care of persons with contagious diseases. Firemen go into burning buildings to save persons trapped by flames. For a good reason we may risk our life to save another.

May we deliberately do anything to shorten our life? The fifth commandment obliges us to take good care of our health. We must not unnecessarily expose ourselves to sickness or accident, or eat or drink too much so as to become sick or injure our health. Does Ann obey the fifth commandment when she visits Marie who is quarantined with typhoid? Does Pauline observe the fifth commandment when she crosses the street only at places where there is a traffic light?

Fighting. "Blessed are the peacemakers, for they shall be called the children of God" (Mt. 5:9). With these words our Lord tells us that we must avoid fighting and quarreling. We should do everything in our power to prevent the things that lead to fighting. We may, however, fight to protect our property; or, if we are attacked, we have the right to defend ourselves. Striking back is not always the best way. Remember, our Lord showed us how to act toward people who are hateful and mean.

Anger. Do you think Cain's first sin was the murder of his brother? From the story we know that he had been angry with his brother. These angry thoughts led to hatred and desire for revenge. Anger is one of the capital sins. It leads to many others. We cannot always avoid feeling angry; but we can always control the angry thoughts which rise in us, especially the desire to harm the offending person.

Christ will always help us to control our anger. Let us look at Him as the soldiers spit in His face, as they strike Him. Remember His patience and ask for the grace to imitate Him.

Anger is not always wrong. Our Lord was angry with the money changers in the Temple and drove them out with a whip because they were making the house of God a den of thieves. Anyone may be justly angry over the breaking of God's laws. Mother may be angry with us when we do wrong. She may scold us and even punish us. Anger becomes sinful as soon as we purposely lose control of our temper, and let it make us say or do anything which breaks God's law. We should be very careful not to let anger become a habit. When a quick-tempered person begins to get angry we should try to be doubly good humored and kind. Sometimes it is wise to leave until his temper cools down and his good sense returns.

Christ was justly angry with the money changers in the Temple.

Hatred. To hate a person means to be his enemy, to try to hurt him, or to wish that evil may happen to him. Hatred is an uglier vice than anger. If we allow hatred to grow until we wish death or serious injury to a person, we are guilty of a serious sin. We know from the story in the Old Testament that the sons of Jacob envied and hated their brother Joseph. They waited for a chance to harm him. You probably recall how one day they threw Joseph into a pit and wanted to put him to death. Years later Joseph repaid this unkind treatment with kindness and love.

How did Christ repay the evil men who treated Him so shamefully? How do we treat such people?

Revenge. The hatred of Joseph's brothers led them to revenge. Revenge means doing an evil to someone because he has harmed us, or we think he has done harm to us. The desire for revenge does great harm to ourselves. It keeps our minds filled with ugly thoughts and affects everything we do. But our Lord said: "Love your enemies, do good to those who hate you, and pray for those who persecute and calumniate you, so that you may be children of your Father in heaven, who makes his sun to rise on the good and the evil, and sends rain on the just and the unjust" (Mt. 5:44–45). In the Our Father we ask God to forgive us as we forgive those who trespass against us. If we do not forgive others, how can we ask God to forgive us? How did Christ repay those who put Him to death?

Drunkenness. Bodily well-being may be seriously harmed by drunkenness. A person who drinks heavily of intoxicating liquor weakens his sense of responsibility. He shortens his life because excessive drinking affects his health. He loses control of his mind and will. Without control of the mind and will, a person becomes like an animal. A drunkard offends God, and causes great sorrow to his family, his country, and to himself. To use liquor with moderation is no sin; it is only excessive drinking that is sinful. But the habit of drinking immoderately is easily formed.

Bad Example. Bad example, or scandal, may cause spiritual injury to another. If we speak or act in a sinful way before a person, we may show him how to sin or encourage him to commit sin. This is displeasing to God because it is helping Satan to lead a soul astray.

Tom, Jack, and Tom's little brother Mark, were playing ball. Jack pitched the ball. Tom swung and missed. He became angry because he thought he was a good batter. Jack pitched again, and again Tom swung and missed. At the third strike, Tom was so angry that he used God's name in vain. Mark saw and heard him get mad. He also yelled a bad name at the pitcher. Tom gave scandal, or bad example, to Mark.

There is another way of giving bad example by word. We may dare someone to do something he should not do. When two boys are angry and almost ready to fight, we should not encourage them to fight.

We can also give bad example by action. This happens when we commit a sin in the presence of others. Those who see it, especially younger children, may imitate us. Our Lord hates all sin, but the sin of scandal is one which He hates especially. "But whoever causes one of these little ones who believe in Me to sin, it were better for him to have a great millstone hung around his neck, and to be drowned in the depths of the sea" (Mt. 18:6).

This terrible threat of our Lord shows how great a sin it is to give scandal. When men commit murder they take the natural, physical life of the body, but when we give bad example or scandal we attack the supernatural, spiritual life of the soul. The one whom we lead into sin may also pass the sin to others, and those others, in turn, may pass it on to a hundred more. Scandal is like putting poison in the water supply of a great city. Nobody knows how many persons may be affected by the poison. The poison of bad example may keep on working for years and years, even after the death of the one who gave the scandal.

Those who have injured others by bad example are obliged to repair the evil as far as possible. If we have in any way encouraged another to sin, we should tell him what we said or did was wicked, and that we are sorry for it. We should try to make up for the bad example by our good behavior and by praying for the person we harmed.

Kindness to Animals. God has placed man above all the animals of the earth and He intends that man should use these animals for His own welfare. We may kill animals for various purposes, but we must avoid torturing or tormenting them. Let us remember always that they are God's creatures.

Saint Francis preaching to the birds

FOR ME TO STUDY

Catechism Lesson

366. Q. What is the fifth commandment?

A. The fifth commandment is: "Thou shalt not kill."

367. Q. What are we commanded by the fifth commandment?

A. We are commanded by the fifth commandment to live in peace and union with our neighbor, to respect his rights, to seek his spiritual and bodily welfare, and to take proper care of our own life and health.

- *How can we take care of our spiritual well-being?*
- *Why are we bound to take care of our bodily life and health?*
- *How can we care for our neighbor's spiritual well-being?*

368. Q. What is forbidden by the fifth commandment?

A. The fifth commandment forbids all willful murder, fighting, anger, hatred, revenge, and bad example.

- *Why is willful murder forbidden?*
- *When does anger become a sin?*
- *What does it mean to hate a person?*
- *What must you do if you have given bad example?*
- *Can you tell the meaning of all these words and use them in a sentence?*

FOR ME TO REMEMBER

1. Life is a divine gift.
2. We must live our lives according to God's plan.
3. We must take care of our own spiritual life and health.
4. We must take proper care of our neighbor's spiritual and bodily well-being.

FOR ME TO DO

1. Ask God for the grace to desire to forgive anyone who harms me.
2. Try to form the habit of saying a short prayer when I am tempted to be angry.

CHAPTER 5
Thou Shalt Not Commit Adultery

LESSON 21

The Sixth Commandment

Did you ever stop to consider how the saints became saints? Saint Stephen loved God so much that he suffered martyrdom for his faith and thus became a saint. Isaac Jogues and his companions went into the wild unexplored regions of North America in order to teach the Native Americans about God. They suffered many terrible hardships during their journeys. The Native Americans treated the "Blackrobes" cruelly. Isaac Jogues was finally killed by the Native Americans and is now known as St. Isaac Jogues.

On June 24, 1950, Pope Pius XII canonized a little girl, Maria Goretti, because she loved God very much. Maria proved her great love for God by keeping the sixth commandment. Maria became a saint by giving up her life rather than committing a sin against purity.

God gave us, too, a body to be the dwelling place of our soul. The Holy Spirit lives in us when we possess sanctifying grace. We have received Christ's Body and Blood in Holy Communion. Our bodies are like tabernacles, therefore, we must keep our bodies pure and holy. We must keep our bodies covered modestly. Those who dress immodestly are the cause of much sinful temptation—they harm others and also themselves.

Which law of God commands us to be pure and modest? You recall that *the sixth commandment of God is: Thou shalt not commit adultery.* Very often this law of God is called the

commandment of purity. Do you agree that this is a good name to remember for the sixth commandment? Yes, because *by the sixth commandment we are commanded to be pure and modest in our behavior.*

When we consider what the sixth commandment warns us against, we recall that *the sixth commandment forbids all impurity and immodesty in words, looks, and actions, whether alone or with others.*

We must avoid all that the sixth commandment forbids. Let us remember that God has created all things good. As long as we use them in the right way they remain good. It is our wrong use of God's gifts that makes them evil and the cause of sin. Therefore, when we speak or listen to impure language, when we act immodestly or impurely, alone or with others, when we dress in such a way as to cause others to have temptations, look at impure books or pictures, go to bad movies or watch them on television, we are using God's gifts in the wrong way and sin against the sixth commandment.

Saint Maria Goretti is an icon of purity. Stained glass window from Fatimakapelle Church located in Austria.

Aids to Purity

God knows that because of original sin, it is not easy for us to do good; therefore He has given us many aids to help us choose what is good and to avoid what is evil. Through prayer we must ask God to help us to be pure. Our Blessed Mother, who was conceived without sin, is a perfect model or example of purity. Mary is always willing and eager to help us to fight our temptations against purity.

We should often call on her and say, "Virgin most pure, pray for us." "Virgin most chaste, pray for us."

The sacraments are a source of grace, and another means of keeping pure. Frequent confession and Holy Communion, especially, strengthen us against sin.

Besides these supernatural helps we also have natural aids to holy purity. Have you ever heard the saying that idle minds are the devil's workshop, and idle fingers his tools? If we keep ourselves busy we allow no time for the devil. Surely we do not wish to have our minds and bodies the helpers of Satan.

We must learn to turn our eyes away from all that is immodest. We should avoid bad company and bravely resist others who try to tempt us or lead us into temptation or sin. We must be pure, modest, and noble. We must never tempt others by our dress, words, or actions.

Here is a story that shows another natural help to purity. James always enjoyed going to the library with his father. From the time he could read he had gone each week, and always went home carrying two and sometimes three books. One evening his father called James. With a smile on his lips he said, "Jimmy, there are some apples in the kitchen. Will you get them and put them into this dish."

Jimmy looked at the dish which was already full and

answered, "But, father, there's no room for any more apples in that dish. What's your joke?"

"No joke, Jimmy," said father. "You're right. The dish is full. You can't get any more apples into it." Then father paused for a moment. "I'm going to tell you something, Jimmy. I am so happy to see you filling your mind so full of good thoughts that there will be no room for bad ones which will harm you." Shall we be like Jimmy?

Jesus Christ loves the virtue of holy purity very much. He chose the Immaculate Virgin Mary to be His Mother. St. Joseph, whom He chose to be His foster father, is often pictured holding a lily, the symbol of purity because he, too, is a model of purity.

FOR ME TO STUDY

Catechism Lesson

369. Q. What is the sixth commandment?

A. The sixth commandment is: "Thou shalt not commit adultery."

- *What virtue does this commandment urge us to practice?*
- *Explain why saints have died rather than sin against purity.*

370. Q. What are we commanded by the sixth commandment?

A. We are commanded by the sixth commandment to be pure in thought and modest in all our looks, words and actions.

371. Q. What is forbidden by the sixth commandment?

A. The sixth commandment forbids all unchaste freedom with another's wife or husband; also all immodesty with ourselves or others in looks, dress, words or actions.

> *Virgin most pure, pray for us. Virgin most chaste, pray for us.*

FOR ME TO REMEMBER

1. The sixth commandment teaches us to be pure and modest in words and acts.
2. God created all things good. They remain good as long as we use them properly.
3. When we use God's gifts in the wrong way we offend Him.
4. I do the devil's work when my dress or actions serve as a temptation to others.
5. Prayer, confession, and Holy Communion are helps to purity.

FOR ME TO DO

1. Say three Hail Mary's each day for purity.
2. In time of temptation against purity make the sign of the cross devoutly.
3. Choose a patron saint to help me keep pure, e.g., St. Agnes, St. Aloysius Gonzaga, St. Maria Goretti.

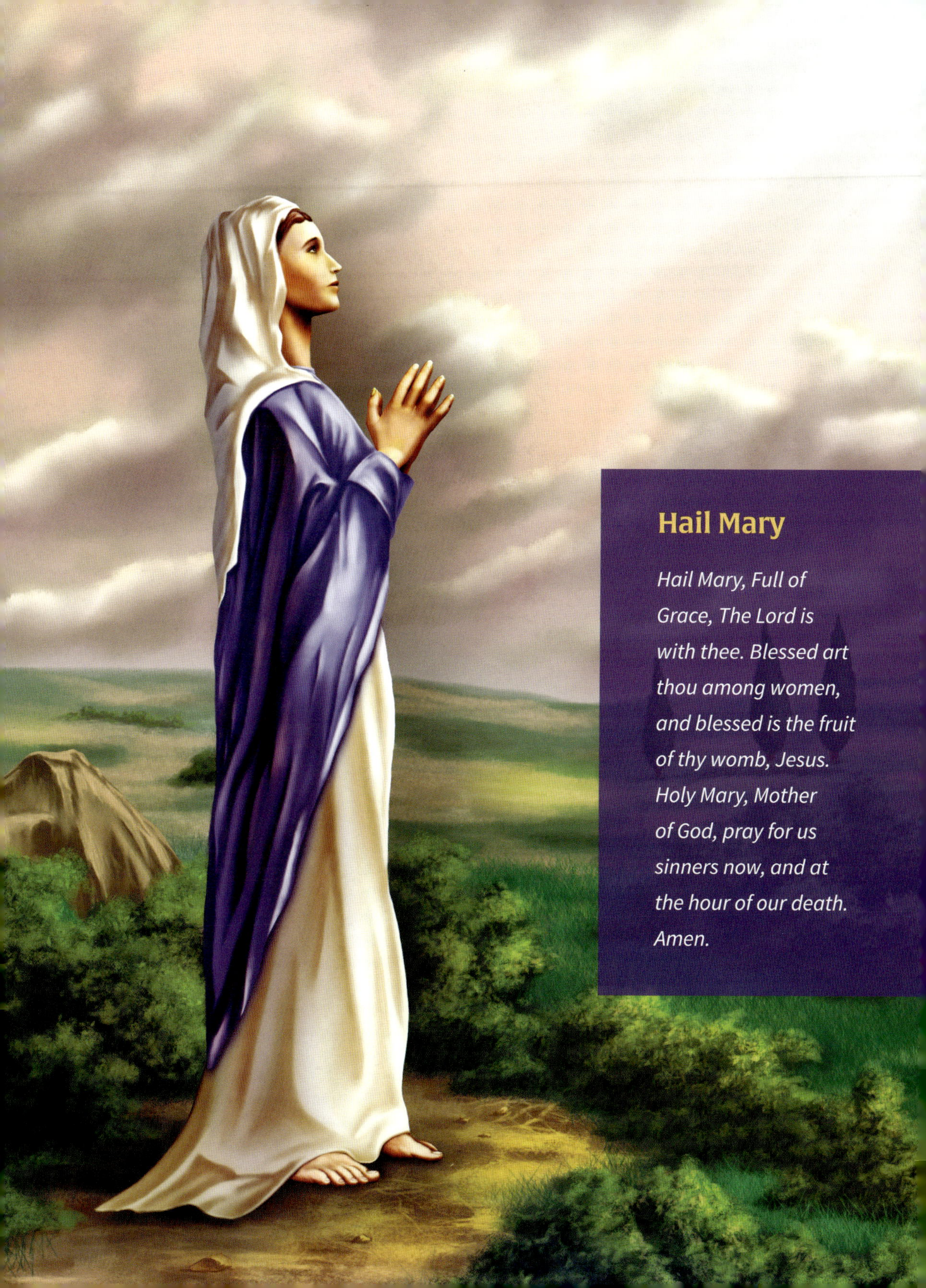

Hail Mary

Hail Mary, Full of Grace, The Lord is with thee. Blessed art thou among women, and blessed is the fruit of thy womb, Jesus. Holy Mary, Mother of God, pray for us sinners now, and at the hour of our death. Amen.

CHAPTER 6
Thou Shalt Not Steal

A group of children was leaving the public library, each of them carrying a book or two. They were talking about the good reading they would have, and how nice it would be to have good books in their own little library. One of the group reminded the others that this was a good chance to practice the seventh commandment which they were studying.

The seventh commandment is: Thou shalt not steal. Do you suppose the child who gave the reminder thought some of the children meant to keep the books? No, but he was probably thinking that by the seventh commandment we are commanded to respect what belongs to others. How truly, then, did these children have a good chance to take care of the library books and keep the seventh law of God.

LESSON 22
The Seventh Commandment

God made the world and everything in it for man. He wishes all men to have enough of this world's goods to be free to think about their immortal souls and their eternal goal. Each man must work to obtain what he needs. He may not take or keep another's goods unjustly. He must not unjustly prevent other

men from getting the money or worldly goods they need to lead the life of a human being. He must not injure his neighbor, or steal, damage, or keep his property, or take away his property rights.

TERMS TO KNOW

- Honesty
- Dishonesty
- Stealing
- Cheating
- Respect

Respect for the Property of Others

Let us think of how we can bring this commandment into our work and play. First of all let us think about the phrase, "respect what belongs to others." When we studied the fourth commandment, we discussed the meaning of the word *respect* in regard to our lawful superiors. Here we are told to respect the property of others. When a friend allows us to use something he owns, he expects us to take care of it and treat it as he would himself. He also expects us to return it to him when we are finished using it.

Barbara owns a bicycle which she treasures. She tells Mary she may have it for a few days because she is going on a trip with her parents. Mary is very grateful and promises to take good care of the bicycle. While Barbara is away, Mary rides the bicycle carefully. She keeps it clean and makes certain to lock it in the garage every night. She is as careful of it as she would have been if it were her very own. When Barbara returns from her trip, Mary brings the bicycle to her. She thanks Barbara and tells her how much she has enjoyed using it. By her actions Mary showed great respect for the property of her neighbor; she kept the seventh commandment.

At home we should respect the property that belongs to other members of our family. This will help us to be honest with people outside of our home. In school we can show respect for the books, playthings, and clothing of our friends. In this way, little by little, we shall build up the right idea about our neighbor's rights to his own property. We shall be pleasing God by trying to be honest at all times.

What advice would you give to a sibling who has the habit of "borrowing" pencils and paper without permission?

What does the seventh commandment forbid? *The seventh commandment forbids all dishonesty, such as stealing, cheating, unjust keeping of what belongs to others, and unjust damage to the property of others.*

Honesty

Honesty is a virtue which makes us pleasing to God. It also makes us pleasing to our neighbor. If we are honest, we can be trusted. Others will be glad to work and play with us because they know we will be fair and honest with them. Persons who are dishonest lose or lessen the love of God. They also lose the trust and friendship of their companions. To be honest is to be noble.

Dishonesty

Stealing is acting dishonestly. It means taking and keeping something that belongs to someone else and making it our own, without the owner's permission or against his reasonable wish. For example, we would sin against the seventh commandment by stealing candy in a store, or by taking our friend's basketball and keeping it as if it were our own. Stealing small inexpensive things often leads to stealing more valuable objects.

Cheating is another form of dishonesty. A storekeeper cheats if he charges unreasonable and unfair prices for his store goods.

Suppose a storekeeper gives us more change than we should get. If we keep the entire amount are we cheating him out of money which is his? When we copy lessons from others we are cheating ourselves more than anyone else. Explain how this is true. Is it cheating to "loaf" on the job?

Some boys and girls think cheating others out of what belongs to them is smart and clever. Others think it is all right to cheat because they see many other people doing it. Let us remember God's law and try to be honest at all times. In His eyes, cheating is never smart or clever.

Unjust keeping of what belongs to others is also a type of dishonesty. Perhaps you have had someone borrow something from you and then keep it. When we ask to use an article belonging to someone else, let us remember to return it.

We are obliged to try to locate the owner of any article of value which we find. Finding a watch, for instance, does not make us the owner of that watch. Your parish usually has a place called the "Lost-and-Found," where lost articles can be brought until the owners claim them. The daily newspapers have a special column in which they advertise lost and found articles. In public buildings you usually will find a special office or room where people may bring articles that have been lost in the building. We are bound by the seventh commandment to make a sincere effort to find the owner of anything of value we might find. Remember that finding a valuable article does not make us the owner of that article. We should take care of it until the owner turns up. If, after reasonable effort and time the owner cannot be found, the article belongs to the finder.

Unjust damage to the property of others is another act forbidden by the seventh commandment. Have you ever sat on a bus and noticed names and initials carved on the seats or other parts of the bus? Have you ever seen furniture in a public building marked in that same way? Have you ever seen bushes and shrubbery in yards or parks ruined because children have broken them? Have you ever seen a child's hat or coat knocked on the floor and stepped on? Have you ever seen schoolbooks soiled and torn because some child used them carelessly? These are only a few of the ways in which we damage the property of others unjustly.

What does the owner of the damaged property have to do? Who usually has to pay for the work and materials needed? Usually the owner does because the dishonest person who caused the damage is also dishonest enough to run away before the damage is discovered.

If a child deliberately damages the property of another and then realizes that he has done wrong, what should he do? He must make up in some way for the damage. This is taught to us in the catechism by the words: *We are obliged to restore to the owner the stolen goods, or their value, whenever we are able.* If we have stolen anything, it is not enough to tell this in confession. Besides confessing the sin, we must also return what we have stolen or repair the damage we have unjustly caused.

Sometimes a person may steal an article and then find later that he cannot return it, even though he wishes to do so. It may have been a toy that has been broken, food that has been eaten, or even a tool that has become worn out. Such a person is bound to restore the value of the article he has stolen or willfully damaged. In case he is unable to do this, he should tell his problem to the priest when he confesses his sin of stealing. The priest will always try to help him. There is a difference between damaging or losing a thing by accident or by our own carelessness.

The virtue of honesty, like every other virtue, should be found in all our actions. Pray that God will help us to live honestly.

FOR ME TO STUDY

Catechism Lesson

373. Q. What is the seventh commandment?

A. The seventh commandment is: "Thou shalt not steal."

374. Q. What are we commanded by the seventh commandment?

A. By the seventh commandment we are commanded to give to all men what belongs to them and to respect their property.

- *Discuss the meaning of the phrase, "respect their property."*

375. Q. What is forbidden by the seventh commandment?

A. The seventh commandment forbids all unjust taking or keeping what belongs to another.

- *Explain why cheating is dishonest.*
- *Why are we bound to try to locate the owner of anything we find?*
- *Discuss how we sin against the seventh commandment by damaging the property of others.*

376. Q. Are we bound to restore ill-gotten goods?

A. We are bound to restore ill-gotten goods, or the value of them, as far as we are able; otherwise we cannot be forgiven.

- *Explain what we should do if we cannot return something we have stolen.*

377. Q. Are we obliged to repair the damage we have unjustly caused?

A. We are bound to repair the damage we have unjustly caused.

FOR ME TO REMEMBER

1. I displease God by cheating, stealing, or unjustly damaging the property of others.
2. I must return things that I borrow.
3. I should ask the priest's advice when I am unable to return stolen goods or their value.

FOR ME TO DO

1. I will be honest in my work and play.
2. I will try to give good example to other boys and girls by always showing respect for the property of others.
3. I will stay away from companions who steal or damage what belongs to other people.

CHAPTER 7

Thou Shalt Not Bear False Witness Against Thy Neighbor

LESSON 23

Speaking the Truth

If someone asked you what you think is the greatest natural gift that God has given you, what would you say? Some of you might answer that you think that the greatest gift is sight, or hearing, or the ability to walk and run, or good health, or even good looks. The answer to that question will always be one for discussion. But did you ever stop to think of, and thank God for the power of speech?

God gave this power to us to help us reveal our thoughts to others. He gave it to us to enable us to help our neighbor and praise God, that through these means we might reach our eternal goal. So important is this gift that God has given us a commandment to safeguard it. The eighth commandment says, *"Thou shalt not bear false witness against thy neighbor."* By this commandment *we are commanded to speak the truth in all things.* To bear false witness means knowingly to say what is untrue, that is, to tell a lie about someone.

The Model of Truth

When Jesus lived here on earth, He said, "I am the Way, the Truth, and the Life" (Jn. 14:6). To live like Jesus we must always speak the truth, act the truth, and live the truth. Sometimes this is not an easy thing to do. It is especially hard to tell the truth when

we have done something wrong and could escape punishment by telling a lie. At such times it takes courage to admit our wrongdoing and to accept our punishment. Our Lord is pleased with children who act truthfully in this way.

On Monday morning your mother tells you that if you can get good grades in arithmetic each week, she will reward you by taking you to your grandmother's who lives out of town. You try your very best because you would like to go. On one day, however, you become a little careless and do not make a good grade. You can see your trip fading away. Suddenly, you remember that you could use the teacher manual to find the right answers. Mother would never know the difference. Would this be honest? Would it be acting truthfully? Christ is your model. What would He do? What would He want you to do?

I am the Way, the Truth, and the Life

What Is a Lie?

When we deliberately deceive another person we tell a lie. It can be done by words, or sometimes by actions. Speech was given to us so that we might express our thoughts. If we do not do so honestly we are guilty of lying. It is a very easy thing to get into the habit of lying, but it is a very bad habit because every lie offends God. No one trusts a boy or girl who tells lies.

An interesting story is told of a boy who liked to fool people. One day while he was swimming he decided to have some fun. He called, "Help, help!" They saw him bobbing up and down and they rushed into the water to save him. When they came closer, he raised his head and laughed, "I fooled you that time!"

A few days later he tried the same prank again. Thinking he might really be in danger, his friends again came to him only to be fooled a second time.

Some time later, when the lad was again in swimming, he got a cramp and found to his surprise he was unable to swim. He called, "Help, help!" When his pals heard him, they said, "He fooled us twice. He won't catch us again." They did not go to his rescue. Their little prankster friend drowned.

Is there ever a time when we are permitted to tell a lie? No, a lie is always wrong. However, we do not have to answer questions about matters which others have no right to know. We may give an evasive answer, that is, one that answers the question without giving the requested information.

What the Eighth Commandment Forbids

The eighth commandment forbids lies and harming the name of another.
"A good name is better than riches" (Prov. 22:1) is an old and famous saying. Everyone has a right to his good name. It is wrong to harm a good name or reputation, as it is called, even if what we say is true. But it is still worse if what we say is not true. A person who does this is usually guilty also of the sin of envy.

The Jews accused our Lord before Pilate of stirring up the nation and refusing to give honor to the emperor. These Jews were jealous of our Lord, and so they lied to ruin His good name.

Rash Judgment

Some people always like to tell why others do things. They watch other people's actions and try to decide why these persons do what they do. Such unkind people often accuse others of doing evil when actually there is no evil involved. This is rash judgment.

Saint Athanasius

Athanasius was forced to flee from his enemies. He entered a small boat and headed up the river. Soon he saw his pursuers in the distance in another boat coming after him. At the next bend he ordered his companions to turn around. As the boats passed, his enemies did not recognize Athanasius in disguise. They called out, "Have you seen Bishop Athanasius?" The saint replied, "He is not far away. If you hurry, you can catch him." Athanasius did not tell an untruth because his words really expressed what was in his mind.

Mary is a girl in the fifth grade. Her mother has been seriously ill. Because she loves her mother very much, Mary goes to Mass and Holy Communion each day to ask our Blessed Lord to make her mother well again. Sue, one of her classmates, notices Mary coming from church every day. It does not take her long to judge that Mary is just trying to make a good impression on her teacher so that she will be chosen to crown our Blessed Mother. What kind of judgment is Sue making? Such judgments about others are called rash judgments, that is, unreasonable or reckless judgments without sufficient foundation. Why do you think Sue began to watch Mary closely? How can Sue make up for any harm she causes? We can readily see how this sin can become very serious. In Scripture, God tells us, "Do not judge, and you shall not be judged . . ." (Lk. 6:37).

If we have harmed the good name of anyone, we are bound to do what we can to make others think well of that person again. We must take back what we have said, if we have lied.

Let us not forget another important matter connected with this commandment. Anyone who listens to stories about others and thereby encourages gossip is also guilty of sin. Why not try to develop the habit of never saying or listening to anything about others unless it is good. Try to say something good about a person when someone else says something against him. No one in this world is as happy as the person who really loves everyone because he truly loves God.

FOR ME TO STUDY

Catechism Lesson

378. Q. What is the eighth commandment?

A. The eighth commandment is: "Thou shalt not bear false witness against thy neighbor."

- *Explain what is meant by "false witness."*

379. Q. What are we commanded by the eighth commandment?

A. We are commanded by the eighth commandment to speak the truth in all things, and to be careful of the honor and reputation of every one.

- *Why is it a serious sin to harm the good name of another?*

380. Q. What is forbidden by the eighth commandment?

A. The eighth commandment forbids all rash judgments, backbiting, slanders, and lies.

- *What is a lie?*

FOR ME TO REMEMBER

1. The gift of speech is given to me that I might express what is in my mind.
2. Christ is my model. I must speak the truth, act the truth, live the truth, and in this way follow Christ, my Leader.
3. "A good name is our most precious possession." Be careful to respect the good name of everyone.
4. We sin against the eighth commandment not only by lying but by telling things about our neighbor that are true but will harm his good name.

FOR ME TO DO

1. Ask God each day to help me love my neighbor because I love Him.
2. Never listen to unkind stories about others even if they are true.
3. Pray today for the grace to tell the truth and accept my punishment if I ever do something wrong.
4. Pray for those whom I have misjudged.

CHAPTER 8

Thou Shalt Not Covet Thy Neighbor's Wife

If we think back to our study of the sixth commandment, we will recall that it commanded us to be pure in our outward behavior. We learned that St. Maria Goretti chose to die rather than commit a sin against purity. The ninth commandment of God is: Thou shalt not covet thy neighbor's wife. The word "covet" means to wrongly wish for, or desire, something that belongs to someone else.

As we study the ninth commandment, we find that by the ninth commandment we are commanded to be pure in thought and in desire. Do you see how these two commandments are alike? Yes, they both direct us to be pure. They are also alike in what they forbid. The ninth commandment forbids all thoughts and desires contrary to chastity. What word has been used here instead of purity?

LESSON 24

Purity of Thought

Have you discovered how these commandments differ from one another? The sixth commandment deals with what we do and say; the ninth commandment deals with what we think and want. In other words, the sixth commandment refers to our external actions; the ninth commandment refers to our inner thoughts and desires. Because our thoughts and desires help us to control our actions, it will help us to be pure and modest if we think pure and chaste thoughts.

Veronica wipes the face of Jesus

We might consider an incident in the story of Christ's suffering and death, which illustrates how our thoughts influence our actions. Think about the holy Veronica. Imagine the beautiful and loving thoughts she must have had in her mind. What courage and faith she must have had in her heart to lead her so bravely to help our dear Saviour. Her courageous thoughts and desires made her brave enough to rush past the soldiers and gently wipe the face of Christ with her veil.

Saint Thomas Aquinas

St. Thomas Aquinas, the patron of education, is known as the Angelic Doctor. He gained this title because he was a very learned man. He also had a great love for chastity. Because he bravely resisted an attempt to make him sin against purity, God gave him special graces to keep him pure and chaste. We can pray to him: "St. Thomas Aquinas, great model of purity, pray for us."

Good thoughts lead us toward good actions. Bad thoughts and desires lead us to bad actions.

Recall from our study of the sixth commandment the supernatural and natural helps to holy purity which God gives us. They will aid us in keeping the ninth commandment too. If we go to confession and Holy Communion often and pray to our Blessed Mother, we have the greatest possible help to remain pure in thought and desire.

We learned that some natural helps to purity are: keeping busy at work or play, staying away from dangerous movies or websites, having good companions, and filling our minds with good thoughts by reading good books.

FOR ME TO STUDY

Catechism Lesson

382. Q. What is the ninth commandment?

A. The ninth commandment is: "Thou shalt not covet thy neighbor's wife."

- *Explain the meaning of the word, "covet"*

383. Q. What are we commanded by the ninth commandment?

A. We are commanded by the ninth commandment to keep ourselves pure in thought and desire.

- *How is the ninth commandment like the sixth commandment?*
- *How is the ninth commandment different from the sixth commandment?*

384. Q. What is forbidden by the ninth commandment?

A. The ninth commandment forbids unchaste thoughts, desires of another's wife or husband, and all other unlawful impure thoughts and desires.

- *Why are thoughts and desires so important?*
- *Explain why St. Thomas Aquinas is called the Angelic Doctor.*

CHAPTER 9
Thou Shalt Not Covet Thy Neighbor's Goods

It is not hard to see that it is wrong to take something which does not belong to us. We learned this in studying the seventh commandment. It is harder to understand that a desire or wish to take something unjustly is also a sin. But this is exactly what the tenth commandment is: Thou shalt not covet thy neighbor's goods.

LESSON 25

What the Tenth Commandment Forbids

Rick is given a pen, a new and rather expensive one. You cannot see why he needs two pens, whereas you have none. Of course, you could use your allowance to buy one, but you prefer to spend your money on movies, soft drinks, or candy. You decide that you can "borrow" one of his pens a few times. Then you can neglect to return it. Rick will soon forget about it and it will become yours. Now whether or not you act on your plan, you have already broken the *tenth commandment*, which *forbids all desire to take or keep unjustly what belongs to another, and it also forbids envy at their success.*

The story of Cain shows how dangerous it is to envy the success of others. Because God was pleased with his brother Abel, Cain brooded and became so jealous that he finally killed him.

Envy is sadness at another person's good fortune or success.

Very often it is the cause of other sins. Sometimes it causes people to speak unkindly of others, thus ruining their good name. Envy of another's good fortune is always wrong and displeasing to God.

Imagine one of your friends gets invited to a game show on television, where she then succeeds and wins a great prize. Because she answers a few questions correctly, which you too could have answered, she is awarded a trip to New York City. Now you have a good chance to congratulate her, or you can give in to the temptation to be envious or to have a feeling of sadness at her good luck. You can even allow such thoughts as, "Why does she have to get all the breaks, she isn't any smarter than I," or "She will look fine in New York; she doesn't even have nice clothes." It would make you so much happier, and her, too, if you were to be the first to tell her how glad you are that she won the prize, and mean it, and how you hope she will have a wonderful time. You might even tell her that if you have anything she would like, you would be happy to lend it to her.

Perhaps the greatest help in keeping this commandment is to learn early in life to be happy and satisfied with what we have, to try to overcome that restlessness of wanting everything we see others have, and to remember that Christ was born in a cave that was not His own and buried in a grave that belonged to another.

When we began the study of the last seven commandments, we wanted to learn how God expects us to love our neighbor. Now we know that by keeping these commandments we live like Christ who is our model and guide.

FOR ME TO STUDY

Catechism Lesson

386. Q. What is the tenth commandment?

A. The tenth commandment is: "Thou shalt not covet thy neighbor's goods."

387. Q. What are we commanded by the tenth commandment?

A. By the tenth commandment we are commanded to be content with what we have, and to rejoice in our neighbor's welfare.

388. Q. What is forbidden by the tenth commandment?

A. The tenth commandment forbids all desires to take or keep wrongfully what belongs to another.

- *Review the seventh commandment.*
- *Tell how the seventh and tenth commandments are related.*
- *Discuss why it is a good thing to go around with boys and girls who have about the same things in life as you have.*

FOR ME TO REMEMBER

1. It is very important for our happiness to be content with what we have.
2. Envy is the cause of many other sins.
3. What I do for my neighbor, I do for Christ.
4. Live always mindful of the presence of God.

FOR ME TO DO

1. Try to see how all I have, has been given to me by God. Thank Him for everything.
2. Ask God for the grace to rejoice always in my neighbor's good fortune.
3. Be the first to congratulate others when they succeed at something.

The Last Seven Commandments of God

Write your answers on a separate sheet of paper

PART I Which commandments tell us to do the following?

1. To love and obey our parents
2. To be truthful at all times
3. To eat proper food and get enough rest
4. To return any article we have borrowed
5. To watch only approved movies and television programs
6. To respect and obey our teachers
7. To give good example to our neighbor
8. To be pure in word and act
9. To try not to fight with companions
10. To be satisfied with the amount of spending money our parents give us
11. To pray to the Blessed Virgin when tempted against purity
12. To try to locate the owner of any article we may find
13. To avoid unkind talk about our neighbor
14. To keep away from companions who lead us into sin
15. To pay for any damage done to the property of others

PART II Completion

Complete the following sentences by filling in the missing words:

1. My body is the temple of the (1).
2. The sixth commandment requires me to be pure in (2), (3), and (4).
3. The fourth commandment tells us that we must (5) and (6) our parents.
4. We must live our lives according to (7) plan.
5. We must take care of our own and of our neighbor's (8) and (9) well-being.
6. The seventh commandment forbids all (10).
7. A great help in keeping the tenth commandment is to be (11) with what we have.
8. The ninth commandment refers to our (12) and (13).
9. We must (14) any damage we have caused unjustly.
10. We sin against the eighth commandment by telling (15).

PART III Multiple Choice

Choose the correct answer:

1. I must love and obey my parents chiefly because:
   A. they will punish me.
   B. they love me and take care of me.
   C. they take the place of God.

2. When parents become old they should be taken care of by the:
   A. children.
   B. Catholic Charities.
   C. city.

3. The fifth commandment forbids:
   A. missing Mass on Sundays.
   B. telling lies.
   C. murder, suicide, fighting, and bad example.

4. Some means of helping us to be pure are:
   A. reading all kinds of comic books.
   B. going to confession and Holy Communion often.
   C. attending any kind of movie.

5. If we have stolen or unjustly damaged another's property we are obliged to:
   A. tell our parents.
   B. restore the goods or their value.
   C. pay for only a part of the damage.

6. If someone is telling an unkind story about another person we should:
   A. try to say something good about that person.
   B. listen attentively to the story.
   C. repeat the story to others.

7. The ninth commandment tells us to:
   A. be just.
   B. be pure in thought and desire.
   C. to speak truthfully.

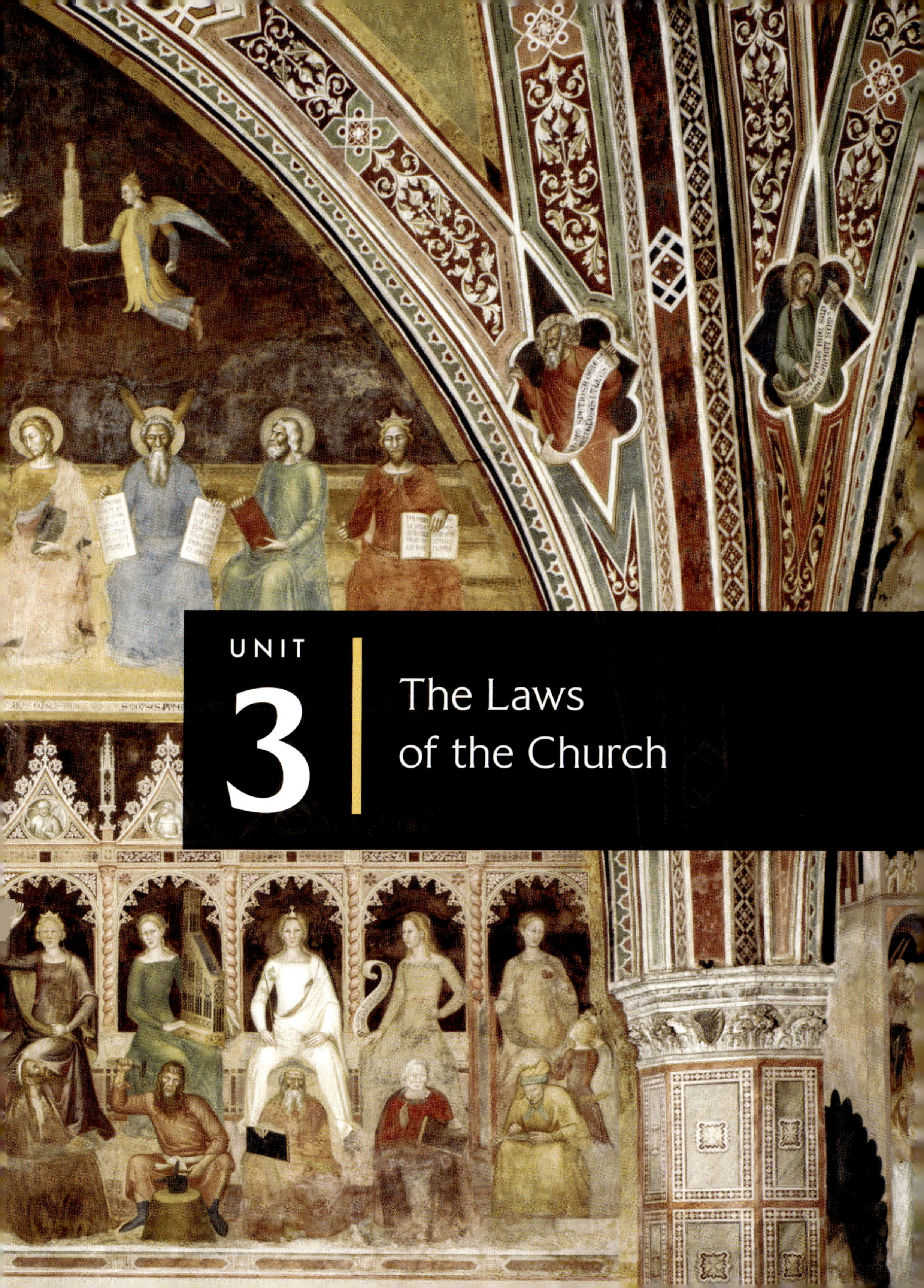

UNIT

3 The Laws of the Church

CHAPTER 10
The Five Precepts of the Church

A young mother and father moved into a new neighborhood. Their house was very nice, but it was on the corner of two busy streets. Since they had three children under four years of age, they decided to build a fence around the back yard. In that way, the children could go outside and play and not be in danger of running into the street and being injured by cars or trucks. Their parents built the fence because they loved them and wanted them to be able to play as safely as possible.

LESSON 26

The Commandments Protect Us

God our heavenly Father, has given us the Ten Commandments as a kind of protective fence to help us love and serve Him on earth and be happy with Him forever after we die. God has also given us the Church to help us during our life on this earth. The Church loves us so she guides, and even punishes us, just as any mother who loves and takes care of her children. For this reason we speak of the Catholic Church as our Holy Mother Church. To shield us from evil and to help us keep the laws of God, Holy Mother Church has given us certain precepts of her own. These are like a protecting fence too.

Christ Himself conferred on the Church the power to give us precepts. Our Lord told the Apostles, "Whatever thou shalt bind

on earth shall be bound in heaven; whatever thou shalt loose on earth shall be loosed in heaven" (Mt. 16:20–21). The Holy Father, and all Catholic bishops are successors of the Apostles. To them also Christ spoke these words.

In addition to these precepts, the Church has made many laws. For example, the Church has declared that a girl who is 14 or younger cannot enter into a valid marriage; there is a law that obligates parents to educate their children both generally as well as in the teachings of the Church. There also are laws about Church music, keeping parish records, guarding the tabernacle key, taking vows, processions, and many other matters. Some of these laws are for bishops, others for priests, still others for Brothers and Sisters. The chief precepts of the Church—which we will now study—are binding on all Catholics who have reached the age of reason (seven):

Precept—a law or command that is considered binding on the faithful.

1. You shall attend Mass on Sundays and holy days of obligation.
2. You shall confess your sins at least once a year.
3. You shall receive Holy Communion at least during the Easter season.
4. You shall observe the prescribed days of fasting and abstinence.
5. You shall help to provide for the needs of the Church.

If the Church has the power to make laws, she also has the power to enforce them. Therefore, the Church has the right to punish those of her members who disobey her.

The Church also has the right to change any law which she has made. She cannot change laws made by God. She can change only those laws made by herself. Sometimes she excuses us from keeping a particular law for a good reason. In such a case the Church is acting just as our mother does when she changes a rule she has made for us. For instance, some mothers will not let children watch television on school nights; they make a rule forbidding it. However, when there is to be a special program, or when the children need recreation, she sets the rule aside for one night. Bishops sometimes excuse Catholics from the law of fast and abstinence when there is a good reason. For example, when a holiday such as the Fourth of July comes on a Friday, the bishops may excuse us from the law obliging us to abstain from meat.

The Church can never change laws made directly by God. Therefore, she can never excuse us from keeping the Ten Commandments of God.

The precepts and laws of the Church help us to keep the commandments of God more faithfully and to live our lives according to the way Christ has taught us. Speaking about His Church, Christ said, "He who hears you, hears Me . . ." (Lk. 10:16). Let us remember these words and always be willing to obey our Mother the Church in all that she commands.

FOR ME TO STUDY

Catechism Lesson

Q. Which are the chief precepts of the Church?

A. The chief precepts of the Church are these five:

1. You shall attend Mass on Sundays and holy days of obligation.

2. You shall confess your sins at least once a year.
3. You shall receive Holy Communion at least during the Easter season.
4. You shall observe the prescribed days of fasting and abstinence.
5. You shall help to provide for the needs of the Church.

- *Who gave the Church power to make laws for Catholics?*
- *May the bishop give us permission to eat meat on certain Fridays?*
- *May the Church change any of the commandments of God?*

FOR ME TO REMEMBER

1. Our Holy Mother Church guides and protects us.
2. The Church has the right to make laws and to change the laws she makes.
3. The Church has the right to punish those who break her laws.
4. The laws of the Church help us to live our lives according to Christ's plan.

FOR ME TO DO

1. Thank God for giving me His Church to help me to live a holy life.
2. Pray often that all men may come to know and love our Holy Mother Church.
3. Keep before my eyes always what the Church requires of me.

CHAPTER 11

Attend Mass on Sundays and Holy Days of Obligation

Not long ago, scientists reported that a total eclipse of the sun would occur in a certain location on a certain day and hour. The whole scientific world was very much interested. Astronomers prepared to obtain photographs and to make careful observations. Many traveled great distances. These scientists were willing to sacrifice comfort, money, and the company of their families in order to see and photograph this wonderful event.

Every day at Holy Mass a far greater marvel takes place. Christ our Lord becomes present upon the altar at the command of one of His creatures, the priest. But how many make any effort to be present every day for this holy sacrifice? Many do not realize how wonderful the Mass really is. To help us understand how necessary it is to worship God in the Mass, the Church has made a law commanding Catholics to assist at Mass on Sundays and holy days of obligation. The first precept of the Church is: You shall attend Mass on Sundays and holy days of obligation. Why does the Church repeat the third commandment of God as her law? Because the command comes partly from God, and partly from the Church. God set the obligation. The Church tells us the day and the manner it is to be observed.

LESSON 27

Holy Days of Obligation

The Church celebrates many holy days. Nearly every day of the year is a feast in honor of Christ, His Blessed Mother, the angels, or of some saint. But the key word here is *obligation*. The *holy days of obligation are the days on which we are obliged or commanded to attend Holy Mass and, if possible, to avoid work.*

The holy days of obligation in the United States are these six:

Christmas Day (December 25)

Mary, Mother of God (January 1)

The Ascension (The Sixth Week of Easter)

The Assumption (August 15)

All Saints' Day (November 1)

The Immaculate Conception (December 8)

Our Lady's *Immaculate Conception* is a beautiful holyday. Of all our Lady's privileges, this one fills her with a special joy. For all eternity Mary will joyously thank God that never for one instant did original sin stain her soul. She always belonged to God, from the first moment of her existence.

This feast is celebrated on ***December 8***. The Blessed Mother, under her title of Immaculate Conception, is the patroness of our United States. Let us often call on her for help and guidance.

December 25—Christmas. "Glory to God in the highest and on earth peace to men of good will" (Lk. 2:14) sang the angels on

Do you know what "transubstantiation" means?

This is the term given to the reality of the bread and wine becoming the Body and Blood of Jesus after the priest consecrates them. The Council of Trent declared: "Because Christ our Redeemer said that it was truly His body that He was offering under the species of bread, it has always been the conviction of the Church of God, and this holy Council now declares again, that by the consecration of the bread and wine there takes place a change of the whole substance of the bread into the substance of the body of Christ our Lord and of the whole substance of the wine into the substance of His blood. This change the holy Catholic Church has fittingly and properly called transubstantiation."

the first Christmas night. The Son of God became man in order to give us our first Christmas gift, Himself.

New Year's Day, *January 1*, is the Solemnity of Mary, Mother of God. We honor Mary in many ways throughout the year, sometimes by considering her glorious Assumption, or on other occasions her queenship. But on *January 1*, we honor Mary as "Mother." She is not just the Mother of Jesus' Humanity, she is also the Mother of his Divinity. This is why we call Mary the Mother of God, because Christ's human and divine natures cannot be separated.

Another holy day honoring our Lord follows the glory of Easter. We know that Christ spent forty days on earth after His resurrection. Then gathering His Apostles together, He bade them a loving farewell. As He was speaking, He slowly rose higher and higher into the heavens until He finally disappeared. As the date for Easter changes, so too, the feast of the *Ascension* is a movable feast. It is always celebrated *forty days after Easter*. So the Ascension always falls on a Thursday, although the celebration of the feast is transfered to the following Sunday in many dioceses.

Christ gave His Mother to be our mother. He most certainly wants us to love and honor her. On *August 15* we celebrate her glorious Assumption. Catholics have always believed that Mary was assumed body and soul into heaven at the end of her life on earth. In 1950, the Church solemnly declared the Assumption a *dogma* of faith, that is, a truth which Catholics must believe.

On *November 1* we honor *all* the *saints* in heaven. Numberless souls have entered heaven since the creation of the world. Some of them were famous and have won much honor and glory in the Church on earth, in addition to the great glory that is theirs in heaven. There are many others, perhaps great ones, who were hidden saints on earth. Their lives gave honor and glory to God, but He did not want them to be known to the world. Then there are other saints, babies who died immediately after Baptism, or souls who just reached heaven by a last minute conversion. All of these souls are precious in the eyes of God. In honoring God's friends we honor Him.

How Do We Keep These Days Holy?

Our first obligation is to worship God by attending the Holy Sacrifice of the Mass.

Years ago there was a terrible persecution in Mexico. Priests had to move about among the people in disguise in order to offer Mass. What a risk for both the priests and the people! But it was worth it. Some of them were caught and became glorious martyrs of Christ, but the Mass continued to be offered. Reflecting on the hardships of these priests should give us gratitude for the ease at which we can attend Mass, and it should also remind us to never take Mass for granted by being fully attentive and present. Ask God to help you be present at Mass with great devotion and attention.

The Mass begins with the Sign of the Cross. To get the full benefit from the Mass and to give God the full amount of worship, we should be in church in time to make the opening Sign of the

Cross with the priest. If we examine our conscience about being late for Mass, we often find that it is due to carelessness, thoughtlessness, or indifference. We could have been on time if we had made an effort to be in church at the right time. If we come into church after Mass has started, we are late. If we are a little late, through our own fault, we commit a venial sin.

> *The Liturgy of the Word is the first principal part of the Mass, which we are obliged to be present for. If we are late to Mass for reasons that could have been reasonably avoided, so that we miss the Liturgy of the Word, we commit a grave sin, unless we make up for it by attending a later Mass.*

A good way to be fully present at Mass is to use the missal and to offer the Mass along with the priest. Then we will not have time to look around or slouch on the kneeler. At the Offertory we can offer ourselves with Christ to God the Father. At the Consecration we can ask God to make us become more like to Christ, ready to go out and live His life in our play, work, and study, no matter the cost.

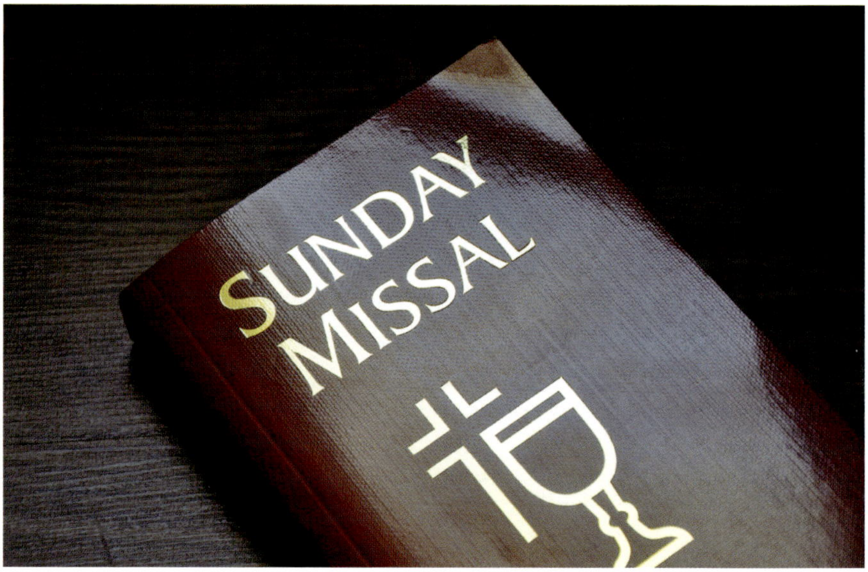

May I be excused from Mass? Yes, but *a Catholic who through his own fault misses Mass on a Sunday or holy day of obligation commits a grave sin*. A serious reason means a very good reason, such as sickness, taking care of the sick, work, or great difficulty or danger. Can you mention others?

When some people go vacation for the summer, or boys and girls go to a certain kind of camp, they may believe they are excused from attending Mass because the Church is far away. Whether they are excused or not depends on the distance and other circumstances. Even during vacation we are bound by the obligation of attend Mass. If our parents select a summer camp for us, we should help them choose a place where there is a Catholic church so we can attend Mass and receive the sacraments.

Some people excuse themselves from going to Mass because they are too "tired" to get up in the morning. Our Lord was tired when He carried His cross. We know He fell under it several times. We should reflect on this on those days that we feel we are too tired to go to Mass on Sundays, or on holy days of obligation.

Work Is Forbidden

The first precept of the Church also *obliges us to abstain from work on holy days of obligation, just as on Sundays, as far as we are able.* It is important to keep these days holy. Only out of real necessity should we do work on Sundays or holy days. Do not try to fool yourself into thinking it is necessary to cut the grass, or wash the car, or do some washing when it really is not. Remember you cannot fool God. Sundays and holy days can also be kept holy by reading Catholic books or newspapers. We can also visit the sick or the lonely and bring cheer to Him who said, "Whatever you do to the least of my brethren you do unto me" (Mt. 25:40).

FOR ME TO STUDY

Catechism Lesson

390. Q. Is it a grave sin not to attend Mass on a Sunday or a holy day of obligation?

A. It is a grave sin not to attend Mass on a Sunday or holy day of obligation unless we are excused for a serious reason. They also commit a grave sin who, having others under their charge, hinder them from attending Mass, without a sufficient reason.

1333. Q. How many holy days of obligation are there in the United States?

A. In this country there are six holy days of obligation, namely, 1) Feast of the Immaculate Conception (Dec. 8th); 2) Christmas (Dec. 25th); 3) Mary, Mother of God (Jan. 1st); 4) Feast of the Ascension of Our Lord (forty days after Easter); 5) Feast of the Assumption of the Blessed Virgin (Aug. 15th); and 6) Feast of All Saints (Nov. 1st).

1334. Q. How should we keep the holy days of obligation?

A. We should keep the holy days of obligation as we should keep the Sunday.

- *What do you mean by holy days of obligation?*
- *Do all the holy days honor Christ?*
- *How should we keep these days holy?*

FOR ME TO REMEMBER

1. In the United States there are six holy days of obligation.
2. We should try to avoid anything that would prevent us from attending Mass on Sundays and holy days.
3. We also keep these days holy by avoiding unnecessary servile work.

FOR ME TO DO

Unite myself with the Holy Mass being offered now.

CHAPTER 12

Confess Our Sins and Receive Holy Communion

LESSON 28

The Second and Third Precepts of the Church

The second precept of the Church is: *To confess our sins at least once a year.* The third precept of the Church is: *To receive Holy Communion during the Easter time.* These two laws about receiving the sacraments were made by our Holy Mother Church in order to keep Catholics from getting careless about their religious duties.

Catholics think of the suffering, death, and resurrection of Christ. They remember that He merited grace for us on Calvary and that He gave us the sacraments to bring this grace to our souls. Faithful Catholics go to confession and Holy Communion often in order to receive God's grace and remain close to Him.

How We Keep the Second Precept of the Church

By the precept to confess our sins at least once a year is meant that we are strictly obliged to make a good confession within the year, but especially if we have a grave sin to confess. Does Holy Mother Church want us to go to confession only once a year? The law says *at least* once a year. The Church teaches us, however, that it is good to go to confession much more often than once a year. People who are sick should not wait until they are dying to call a doctor. Neither should we wait to go to confession until we have committed a mortal sin. Frequent confession will increase sanctifying grace within our souls, will strengthen us against

temptation, and will help us live closer to almighty God.

How We Keep the Third Precept of the Church

We keep the second precept of the Church by going to confession any time during the year. To keep the third precept, however, we must receive Holy Communion during the Easter time. *Easter time* begins on Easter Sunday and ends 50 days later on the Feast of Pentecost. Just as our Lord rose gloriously on Easter Sunday, so Holy Mother Church wants her children, during this holy season, to rise from sin. A *Catholic who neglects to receive Holy Communion worthily during the Easter time commits a grave sin.*

The Church commands us by law to receive Holy Communion once a year, but through all the centuries she has invited and urged us to receive

First Communion

Long ago, children were not permitted to receive our dear Lord until the age of twelve or thirteen. Pope St. Pius X changed the law and permitted little children who had reached the age of reason to make their First Holy Communion. The Church then urged all the faithful to receive Holy Communion monthly, weekly, or even daily.

Holy Communion much more often than that.

In order to receive Holy Communion worthily we must have the right intention. We must be free from mortal sin. We must observe the Eucharistic Fast. It is important to open our hearts to Christ's presence and to make our souls a beautiful dwelling place for our Lord.

These are the regulations for the Eucharistic Fast:

1. We must abstain for one hour from solid foods.
2. We must abstain one hour from all other beverages except water. Water never breaks the Eucharistic Fast.

The special privilege for the sick, old, or infirm people is: They may take medicine, in liquid or solid form before Holy Communion, without any limit.

Our Holy Father urges all who can to observe the old form of the Eucharistic Fast, that is fasting from midnight, as much as possible.

If a person is convicted of mortal sin, he may not receive Holy Communion without first going to confession. An act of perfect contrition is not sufficient. But venial sins need not keep us from Holy Communion. An act of contrition and a fervent Holy Communion will cleanse our soul from all venial sins for which we are sorry. It is not necessary to go to confession every time we wish to receive the Holy Eucharist. If we are free from mortal sin we may receive as often as we wish. However, we should confess regularly if we receive regularly—every week, two weeks, or at least once a month.

All Catholics do not appreciate the wonder and power of this great sacrament. Neither did all the people who lived at the time of Christ and heard Him promise to give Himself in the Holy Eucharist. The Gospel tells us that when the disciples heard Jesus insist that those who will have eternal life must eat of his flesh, that ". . . many of His disciples turned back and no longer went about with Him." (Jn. 6:66) But when Christ turned to His Apostles and asked if they also wished to go away Peter answered, "Lord, to whom shall we go? Thou hast the words of everlasting life . . ." (Jn. 6:69–70). Let us repeat these words of Peter and show Christ our love by frequently receiving Him in the Holy Eucharist.

FOR ME TO STUDY

Catechism Lesson

1349. Q. What is meant by the command of confessing at least once a year?

A. By the command of confessing at least once a year is meant that we are obliged, under pain of mortal sin, to go to confession within the year.

- *Why does the Church want us to go to confession frequently?*
- *Why is it good for the person with no mortal sin to still go to confession?*

1353. Q. What sin does he commit who neglects to receive Communion during the Easter time?

A. He who neglects to receive Communion during the Easter time commits a mortal sin.

- *How often should we go to Holy Communion?*

FOR ME TO REMEMBER

1. All Catholics are advised go to confession at least once a year.
2. To lead a holy life we must go to confession frequently.
3. The Church wants her children to receive Holy Communion frequently.

FOR ME TO DO

1. Pray the Angelus devoutly today for sinners who have not made their Easter duty.
2. Receive Holy Communion for those who fail to make their Easter duty.
3. Invite friends to go to confession and Communion with me, especially those who may not attend regularly.

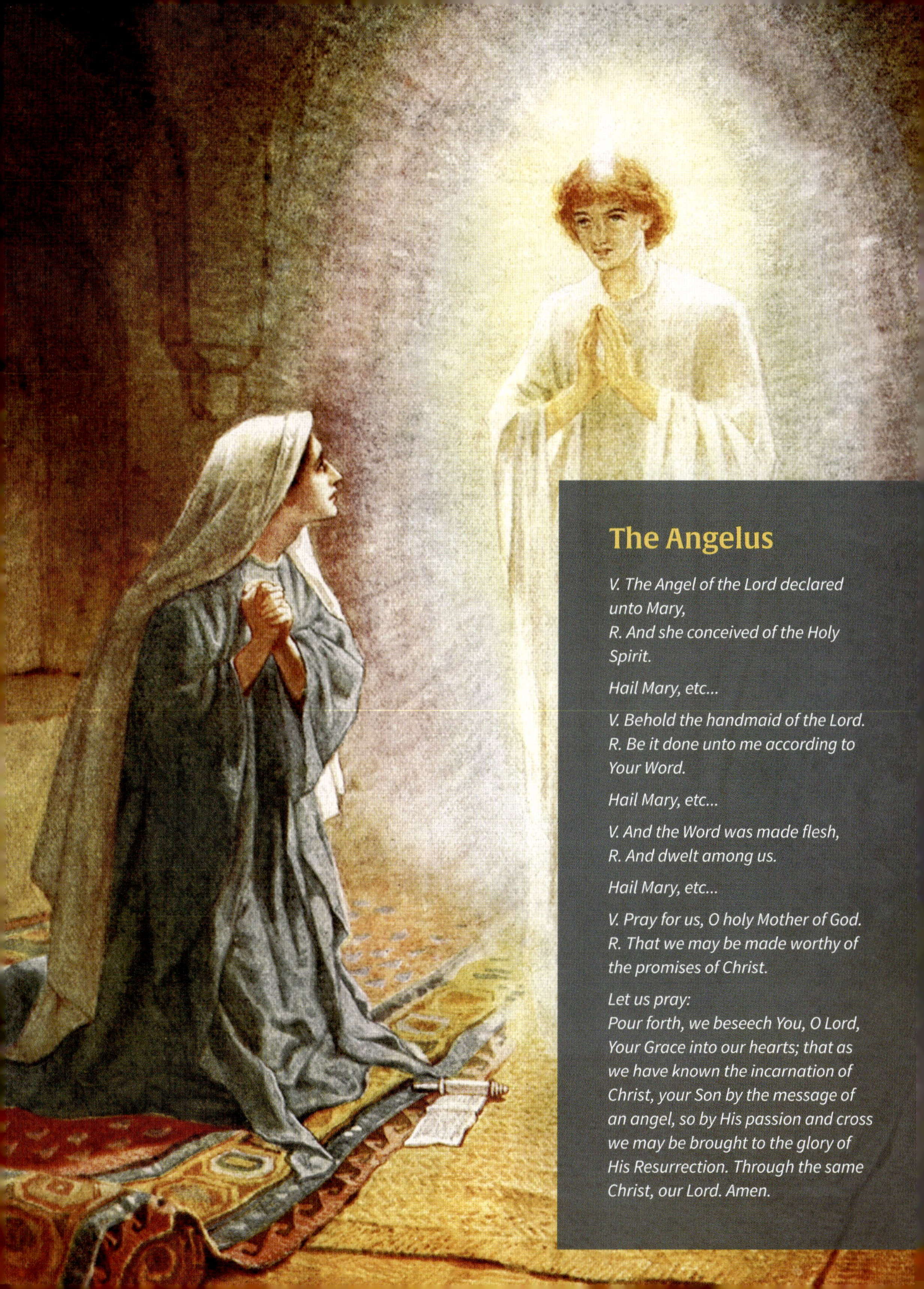

The Angelus

V. The Angel of the Lord declared unto Mary,
R. And she conceived of the Holy Spirit.

Hail Mary, etc...

V. Behold the handmaid of the Lord.
R. Be it done unto me according to Your Word.

Hail Mary, etc...

V. And the Word was made flesh,
R. And dwelt among us.

Hail Mary, etc...

V. Pray for us, O holy Mother of God.
R. That we may be made worthy of the promises of Christ.

Let us pray:
Pour forth, we beseech You, O Lord, Your Grace into our hearts; that as we have known the incarnation of Christ, your Son by the message of an angel, so by His passion and cross we may be brought to the glory of His Resurrection. Through the same Christ, our Lord. Amen.

CHAPTER 13
Fast and Abstain on Days Appointed

LESSON 29

Fasting and Abstinence Are Necessary

The fourth precept of the Church is: You shall observe the prescribed days of fasting and abstinence.

Christ Himself taught us that fasting is good for the soul. He began His public life with a fast of forty days and nights in the desert. He spent this time alone, in prayer and fasting. He was not really alone, however; He had talked with His Father. But someone else was watching Him, too. It was Satan. When the fast was ended, Christ was greatly weakened. Satan was sure he could easily conquer this unusual man. With sly cunning he approached Him. "If you are the Son of God," he said, "command this stone to become a loaf of bread." Jesus quickly said to the tempter: "Not by bread alone shall man live, but by every word of God" (Lk. 4:4).

When Jesus chose His followers, He let them know that they had to train themselves to overcome their weaknesses. He told them, "If anyone wishes to come after me, let him deny himself and take up his cross and follow me" (Mt. 16:24). "To deny ourselves" means to do without things we like; it means to give up things that might keep us from following closely after Christ; it means to choose the hard things, not because we like hard things, but because we love God better than ourselves. Because

When Christ fasted for forty days and nights, he taught us that fasting is good for the soul

we must train ourselves to conquer our wayward tendencies, we must form the habit of practicing virtues.

Obtaining virtue might be difficult at first, but just like training for a sport or practicing an instrument, virtue becomes easier over time and can even bring us joy and pleasure. Think how good it feels to finally be able to play Beethoven's *Fur Elise* on the piano after years of practice. Or what great joy we feel when we finally hit a home run in baseball. Virtue too should eventually be sweet for us—waking up early, making our beds, saying our prayers, all these become less difficult, and more pleasurable, the more often we do them. However, as these things become easier to us, it is important to occasionally take on a more difficult task to keep our mind, body, and soul on the narrow path; this we do when we fast.

Fast and Abstinence

We can be His followers only if we train ourselves. The fourth precept of the Church tells us a way to do this. *It commands us to fast and to abstain on the days appointed.* "To fast" means to eat less food than we usually do. "To abstain" means to keep from doing something, and in the Church law it means to keep from eating meat. We must fast and abstain according to the general precepts of the Church and any special rules of our own diocese.

Fast Days

A fast day is a day on which only one full meal is allowed. Two other small meals may be eaten but the two together must be *less* than the one full meal. The days of fast are Ash Wednesday and Good Friday. On days of fast Catholics may not eat between meals, but they are allowed to take liquids such as milk and fruit juices.

The law of fast is for people between the ages of eighteen and fifty-nine. It is not for children because they need food to grow. It is not for people who are old or sick, or who have to work hard. The Church is a kind mother: she always takes care of the needs of her children.

The law of fast does not bind boys and girls. But we must all do some penance. What, then, can we do to make us strong spiritually? At mealtime, perhaps there is something on the table we like. How can we make a sacrifice that will make our wills strong? What else can we do at mealtime that will not hurt us? We can also sacrifice other things beside food. Can we skip our favorite television program, or give up some of our playtime or funny books? What else?

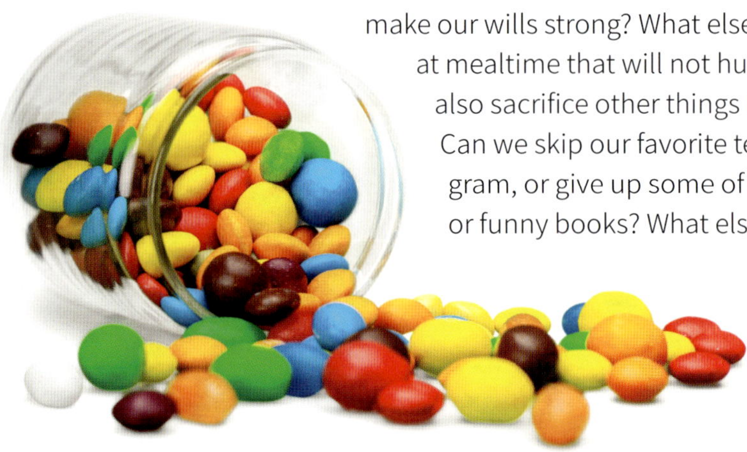

Days of Abstinence

The law of fasting tells us how much food we may eat on certain days. The law of abstinence deals with the kind of food we eat. *A day of abstinence is a day on which we are not allowed the use of meat. All baptized persons fourteen years of age or over who have attained the use of reason are obliged to observe the abstinence days of the Church, unless excused or dispensed.*

Fridays are days of *abstinence*, unless the Friday falls on a solemnity, and so are *Ash Wednesday* and *Good Friday*. On Fridays outside of Lent, some other penance may be substituted for abstinence.

Do you remember why the Church chose Friday as a day of abstinence? It was on that day that Jesus died on the cross. What a marvelous thing to do for us! By fasting and abstaining we can help to make up for our sins at least in a small way. When we go to Mass let us not forget to unite our little sacrifices with Christ's infinite Sacrifice. Then our sacrifice becomes big, too.

TERMS TO KNOW

- Fasting
- Abstinence

FOR ME TO STUDY

Catechism Lesson

393. Q. What do you mean by fast days?

A. By fast days I mean days on which we are allowed but one full meal.

1338. Q. Is it permitted on fast days to take any food besides the one full meal?

A. It is permitted on fast days, besides the one full meal, to take two other small meals, to maintain strength, according to each one's needs. But together these two small meals should not equal another full meal.

394. Q. What do you mean by days of abstinence?

A. By days of abstinence, I mean days on which we are forbidden to eat flesh-meat, but are allowed the usual number of meals.

1339. Q. Who are obliged to fast?

A. All persons over eighteen and under fifty-nine years of age, and whose health and occupation will permit them to fast

- *Why does the Church command us to fast and abstain?*
- *What does the Church want boys and girls to do instead of fasting?*
- *Why are Fridays days of abstinence?*

Match these words or phrases with the correct definitions:

A. fast	1. the age for fasting
B. abstain	2. to do without meat
C. fourteen years of age	3. to eat one full meal a day
D. eighteen to fifty-nine years of age	4. the age at which one must begin to abstain

FOR ME TO REMEMBER

1. The Church commands me to abstain from meat on Friday to thank Christ for dying for my sins.
2. The Church expects children to make small sacrifices for Christ during Lent; she does not ask children to fast.
3. Interior penances are better than exterior penances.

FOR ME TO DO

1. Offer to God something I might do but choose not to because of Him.
2. Look at the crucifix and thank God for dying for us.
3. Remember the days of fast and abstinence.
4. Receive the sacramentals: candles, blessing of my throat, ashes.

CHAPTER 14
Contribute to the Support of the Church

The fifth precept of the Church obliges us to contribute to the support of the Church. *In the early days of the Church, the people brought gifts to be offered at Holy Mass. Some brought bread or wine for the sacrifice. Others brought fruit, vegetables, meat, or articles of clothing. Each person carried his gift up to the altar. The priest took enough bread and wine for that day's Mass. He put aside what he needed to support himself. The rest was given to the poor. That is why the priest still washes his hands at the Offertory.*

LESSON 30

All of Us Must Help

Today many parishes are so large that a procession would take a long time. Large city parishes would not be able to have five and six Masses on Sunday morning, and some people might be forced to miss Mass. So, instead of bringing a gift, each Catholic makes a contribution of money to the collection taken up during the Offertory. The pastor then uses this money to pay the expenses of the church. The adult members of a parish are encouraged and obliged *to contribute to the support of the Church, which means to help pay for the financial expenses of the Church.*

The pastor uses the collection money in many ways. He builds and repairs the church, school, parish house, and other buildings necessary for the parish. He buys sacred vessels,

vestments, wine and altar breads used for Holy Mass. Some of the money supports the school and the sisters who teach there. Each parish also helps to support Catholic Charities which care for the poor, the sick, orphans, and the elderly. Some money is also used for missionary efforts, to help spread the Gospel to those who may have not heard of the salvation given to us by Jesus Christ. When we think of all these activities, we can understand why a pastor needs the generous offerings of the faithful in order to carry on the work of Christ.

Each Catholic makes a contribution of money to the collection taken up during the Offertory. This is used to pay the expenses of the church.

Catholics who can afford to sometimes make special gifts to the Church. For instance, they make donations of sacred vessels, vestments, candles, or furnishings for the Church. Some people make wills and leave money to the Church or to Catholic education. Other people who do not have very much money show their generosity by giving of their time and service. Some of them help their pastor by making needed repairs on the building, by helping to clean the church, by managing clubs for boys and girls, or by taking part in the various activities of the parish.

How We Can Help

This obligation is chiefly for grown people, but children can also help. Most of us can make an offering of money from the little we might earn during the week or out of our allowance. We can also be careful of church property by not damaging it and by helping to keep the school grounds clean. It is well to remember here to respect church property, such as books, desks, or the playground. We are helping our parish when we take good care of its property.

How generous must we be? Christ never looks at the amount in the envelope. Because He is God He looks at the heart of each one of us. He looks to see how great our sacrifice is. He is pleased when He sees that we make our offering with a generous heart. The story of the widow's mite reminds us of this. Do you know the story?

One day Christ sat in the temple watching the people bring in their offerings. A very poor widow came in. She put her offering of a penny into the box and quickly went away. Our Lord turned to His Apostles and told them that this woman had given more than all the rest. Why? She gave all she had.

Let us try to make our offerings to the Church in the same manner. Whether we are rich or poor, let us give to God with love according to our means.

The widow's mite. "She of her want cast in all she had, even her whole living" (Mk 12:44).

FOR ME TO STUDY

Catechism Lesson

1357. Q. Where did the duty of contributing to the support of the Church and clergy originate?

A. The duty of contributing to the support of the Church and clergy originated in the Old Law, when God commanded all the people to contribute to the support of the temple and of its priests

How does the priest use the money given at Mass?

How can a child keep the obligation to support the Church?

How should we make our offering to the Church?

FOR ME TO REMEMBER

1. Christ looks not at the amount given, but at our heart when we put our offering in the collection.
2. Everyone must contribute his share according to his means.

FOR ME TO DO

1. I will be careful of all Church property.
2. I will try as best I can to put something into an envelope on Sunday for the offertory collection.
3. I will help my parish in every way I can.

CHAPTER 15
Observe the Laws of Marriage

After God created Adam He said: "It is not good for man to be alone" (Gen. 2:18). Then God created Eve and gave her to Adam and told the two of them to live as one. This was the first marriage.

Thousands of years passed. Because of original sin, marriage was not always kept sacred. Some men had many wives. Some men treated their wives as animals. Some wives were not good to their husbands. Then Christ came. Once again He showed how God loves marriage. He made marriage even more sacred by making it a sacrament. His first miracle was worked at the wedding feast at Cana.

LESSON 31

What the Church Requires For Marriage

Christ's Church always follows in the footsteps of the beloved Master. Holy Church gave us a commandment to protect the sacredness of Matrimony. *The requirement of the Church is: To observe the laws of the Church concerning marriage.*

What are these laws? *The ordinary law of the Church to be observed at the wedding of a Catholic is this: A Catholic can be married only in the presence of an authorized priest and two witnesses.* By an "authorized priest" is meant the parish priest, that is the pastor, or another priest to whom this right has been given. The two witnesses should be good, practicing Catholics.

This means that they should be Catholics who assist at Mass on Sundays, receive the sacraments, and try faithfully to keep the commandments of God and the Church.

The Church strongly discourages Catholics to marry non-Catholics. If we think of our Church as a kind and protecting mother, we can understand why she does this. If a Catholic marries a non-Catholic, he is placing his own faith in danger. The non-Catholic person sometimes cannot understand the other person's religion and may criticize and complain about it. Because of this some Catholics give up their faith, stay away from Holy Mass and the sacraments, and may even lose their souls. Our Church tries to warn us against this when she advices us not to marry non-Catholics.

The Catholic Church has another reason for discouraging her children to marry non-Catholics. Children need two Catholic parents who agree upon the Catholic training of their children. They must work together to bring up their children in the love and service of God.

In a country like ours, Catholics and non-Catholics are very often together in much of their everyday life. As a result, it may happen that a Catholic may wish to marry a non-Catholic, although the Church discourages it. Under certain conditions the bishop may give a special permission, called a dispensation, for this kind of marriage. The non-Catholic

must promise to allow the Catholic to practice his religion and to raise all children as Catholics. Such a marriage is called a mixed marriage.

Catholics can best obtain God's blessing on their marriage by being married at a *Nuptial Mass*. This Mass has special prayers begging God's blessings for the newly married couple. If people are married during Lent or Advent, they may not celebrate their wedding with any outward show or ceremony, and the Nuptial Mass cannot be said during that time. However, bishops have power even to allow Nuptial Masses at forbidden times.

FOR ME TO STUDY

Catechism Lesson

1037. Q. Why does the Church discourage the marriage of Catholics with persons who have a different religion or no religion at all?

A. The Church discourages the marriage of Catholics with persons who have a different religion, or no religion at all, because such marriages generally lead to indifference, loss of faith, and to the neglect of the religious education of the children.

How did Christ show the importance of marriage?
Why should Catholics marry Catholics?
Why does the Church discourage mixed marriages?

Use these words in a sentence to show their meaning:

Matrimony
dispensation
nuptial blessing
mixed marriage
authorized priest
Nuptial Mass

FOR ME TO REMEMBER

1. God blessed the first marriage in Paradise.
2. Thousands of years later, Christ made marriage a sacrament.
3. The Church gives Catholics a special blessing when they are married at a Nuptial Mass.
4. Children need the help of two Catholic parents to grow up to be good Catholics themselves.

FOR ME TO DO

1. Say a prayer of thanksgiving for my parents.

The Precepts of the Church

Write your answers on a separate sheet of paper

PART I Which precept of the Church is kept in each of these cases:

1. We help around the church or school property without pay.
2. We don't eat meat on Friday.
3. We attend Mass on Sunday.
4. We give money to the Church.
5. Grown people eat only one full meal on certain days.
6. We attend Mass on All Saints' Day.
7. We receive Holy Communion during the Easter time.
8. We make a good confession at least once a year.
9. We give money to Catholic Charities.

PART II Match the following:

Column I	Column II
A. November 1	1. Age for fasting.
B. Assumption	2. No meat may be eaten.
C. Ascension Day	3. A day on which we must assist at Mass.
D. Easter time	4. Forty days after Easter.
E. Vigil	5 To eat only one full meal.
F. 18–59	6. Feast of All Saints.
G. Fast Day	7. Mary was taken up into heaven.
H. Day of abstinence	8. The day before a feast.
I. Holy day	9. First Sunday of Easter to Pentecost.

UNIT

4 The Seven Sacraments

CHAPTER 16

The Seven Sacraments

If you were to place a rock in your back yard, could it of itself be able to change in any way? No, it would remain in the same spot and look just about the same day after day. If your father planted a rosebush in your yard, would it of itself be able to change in any way? It would grow larger and in time it would bear sweet-smelling flowers. God gave plants a power He did not give to the rock. What is that power? If you put your dog in the back yard, would he remain in the same spot like the rock? No, he would jump and run and want you to play with him. God gave animals the same power He gave to plants plus the greater power to move about. Then, if your mother placed your little brother in the yard, would you probably have to stay with him? No doubt you would, because he would want to play and talk with you, and think of things to do. What power has God given to your little brother that the plants and animals did not have? Your little brother can think and talk, and wish or desire.

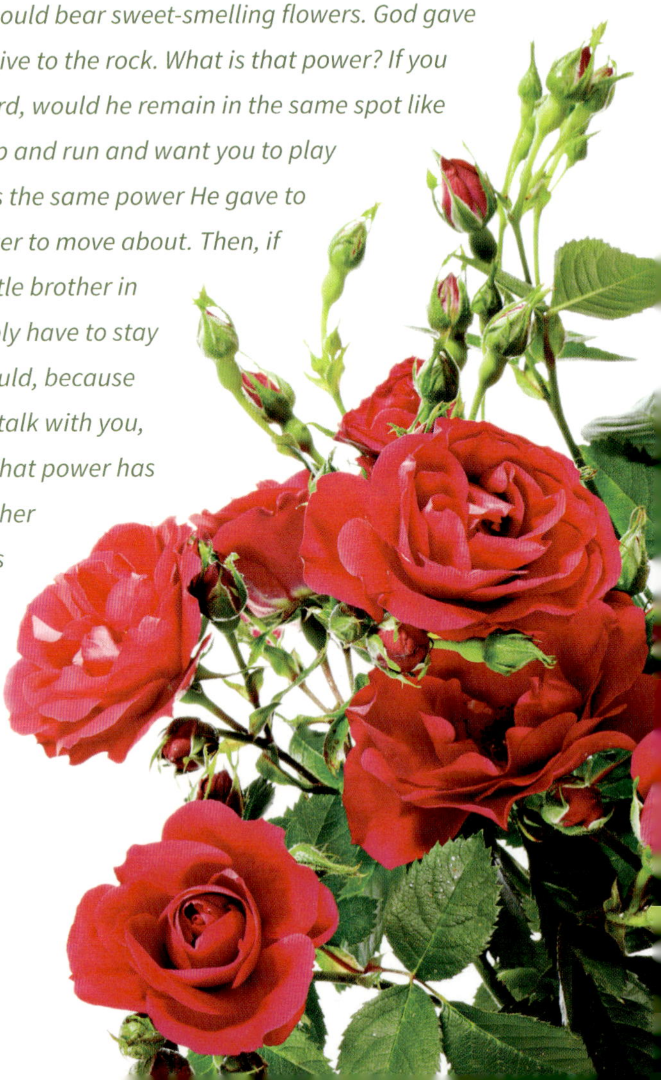

LESSON 32

A Means of Grace

Christ Merited Grace for Us

Besides the natural powers of walking, thinking, talking, willing, God has given those of us who have been baptized a new nature with even greater powers, *supernatural powers.* He has done this because He loves us and wants us to live with Him forever in heaven. Our natural life is nourished and strengthened by healthy foods. What does God give us to nourish and strengthen our supernatural life? God gives us the graces which were merited by His Son, Jesus Christ.

Let us recall what we already know about grace. There are two kinds of grace. What are they? What does sanctifying grace do for us? How does actual grace help us? How can we obtain these graces?

How We Obtain Grace

Jesus Christ not only merited the graces for us, but He also gave us valuable ways to obtain these graces. You have already made use of some of the principal ways of obtaining grace. What are they? You were baptized. You go to confession. You receive Holy Communion. In other words, you have received grace through the sacraments. This year we are going to study the seven wonderful sacraments which Christ in His great love has given to us.

Corporal and Spiritual Realities

Unlike the angels, we have bodies. We are a combination of spirit and matter; we are corporeal (meaning "bodily") and spiritual (meaning our souls) creatures. The sacraments mirror this in that they have spiritual graces that feed our soul, but God uses physical matter to transmit his grace to us.

You already know that the sacraments were given to us by Christ, and that they give grace. You also know that the grace which the sacraments give actually comes to us from Christ. He gained this grace for us when He suffered and died on Calvary. Christ is actually the source of all grace.

Christ knew how necessary it was for us to share in His infinite grace, so He used created things to bring us His grace. This humbles us, assures us we have received His grace, and makes the sacraments more attractive to us.

Christ directed His Church to teach us how to use these created things to obtain the grace He promised. For instance, we must use water to receive the grace of Baptism. We must go to a person, the priest, in confession to have our sins forgiven and receive the grace of Penance and Reconciliation. Can you think of other created things which Christ chose to use as instruments to give us His grace?

There is one more point to remember. The sacraments are outward signs. That is, they are visible. They show outwardly what the sacrament does for us in an invisible, supernatural way. As an example we might use the sacrament of Holy Eucharist. When we receive Holy Communion, we can see the consecrated Host, which is the Body of Christ. We receive the Body and Blood of Christ and know that it is nourishment for our supernatural life, even though the actual effect of Holy Communion is invisible to us. When we put these facts together, we see that *a sacrament is an outward sign instituted by Christ to give grace.*

The Sacraments Give Sanctifying Grace

From our previous study, we also know that *there are seven sacraments: Baptism, Confirmation, Holy Eucharist, Penance and Reconciliation, Anointing of the Sick, Holy Orders, and Matrimony.* In answer to the question, do the sacraments give sanctifying grace, we reply that *the sacraments do give sanctifying grace,* or increase it when it is present.

We mentioned in the first unit of our book that sanctifying grace makes us holy and pleasing to God; makes us adopted children of God; makes us temples of the Holy Spirit and brings God to dwell in our souls. It makes us like God and gives us the right to heaven. It might be well for us to stop here and discuss each of these effects of sanctifying grace. Remember, too, that each time we receive any of the sacraments, sanctifying grace is increased or restored, as the case may be. When is it increased? Restored?

Sacramental Grace

In addition, *each of the sacraments also gives a special grace called sacramental grace.* This is a special grace which helps us fulfill the purpose of the particular sacrament we have received. For example, the sacrament of Confirmation strengthens the virtues we received at Baptism making us more able soldiers of Jesus Christ. The sacramental grace for this sacrament is the special supernatural help which enables us to act and live like a soldier of Christ. Sanctifying grace is the same for each sacrament; sacramental grace is different for each sacrament. Sanctifying grace remains in the soul; sacramental grace comes and goes as we need it.

An example may help you to understand better what sacramental grace is. Perhaps you have a chemistry set, or you may have used one with someone else. Such a set contains many bottles and envelopes. Each of these is filled with a particular liquid or solid. With your chemistry set you received a book of directions. You are told exactly how to use each chemical. You are warned against using it in any other way because it produces its results only if it is used in the proper manner. It is not possible to get the same result from any other chemical.

Just as each chemical produces a special effect, so too, each sacrament gives its own special sacramental grace. This grace helps us to gain supernatural help from each of the seven sacraments. The book of directions with the chemistry set assured you that if you used each chemical exactly according to the directions, it would produce the effect you wanted. Accordingly, *the sacraments always give grace if we receive them properly*. They give sanctifying grace. They give sacramental grace.

A special preparation is required for each sacrament. We will learn what this preparation is when we study each of the sacraments. For all of the sacraments, however, we must have the intention of receiving the sacrament and of obtaining the grace which the sacrament gives. This is what we mean when we say the sacraments always give grace if we receive them properly.

Sacraments of the Dead

Have you ever tried to turn on the lamp light in your living room and found that it would not work? Did you then try to discover the cause of the trouble? Let us suppose you did and you found that the electric cord was not connected to the outlet. You plugged it in and turned on the light. Immediately the lamp lit up. Why did the lamp fail to give the light when it was disconnected? Was the wire in the cord dead? No, it was not dead, but because it was cut off from the main power line, the electricity was not able to pass into it. While it was disconnected, the bulb was unable to produce any light. It was unable to do any good.

Will your soul ever die? No, you learned a long time ago that your soul will live forever; it will never die. Your soul is *immortal*. But the supernatural life of the soul, that is, the new nature given at Baptism, the life of grace in the soul, can be lost. How were Adam and Eve punished when they sinned against God? You remember that they lost sanctifying grace. What do some people do today to cause almighty God to punish them the same way He punished Adam and Eve? Yes, they commit mortal sin. Mortal sin, as it were, breaks the connecting line between God and the soul. As long as the connection is broken, the soul is without sanctifying grace. The soul no longer has the life of grace.

Christ gave us two sacraments through which we can regain the life of grace lost through sin. You know the names of both of them. Most of you received one of them when you were babies. When you received Baptism you received sanctifying grace for the first time. The divine life of God Himself came into your soul. The other sacrament which restores sanctifying grace if it has been lost through sin is the sacrament of Penance and Reconciliation.

These two sacraments, Baptism and Penance and Reconciliation, are called sacraments of the dead. Can you think why the Church gave them this name? Recall why we receive Baptism. Baptism takes away original sin which deprives our soul of sanctifying grace. When we go to confession with a mortal sin on our soul, we know that Penance and Reconciliation will give back the life of sanctifying grace. *Baptism and Penance and Reconciliation are called sacraments of the dead because their chief purpose is to give the life of grace to souls dead through sin.*

Sacraments of the Living

Christ gave us some sacraments whose purpose it is to give the life of grace to our souls. He has also given us sacraments which will increase and strengthen the life of grace which we already have. One of these you often receive when you assist at Holy Mass, the Holy Eucharist. Besides the Holy Eucharist, there are four other sacraments which increase and strengthen our supernatural life. What sacrament makes us soldiers of Christ? Which sacrament did your father and mother receive when they were married? Before priests are able to offer Mass, they must receive a special sacrament. What is the name of the sacrament that made them priests? Which sacrament does the priest give to people who are in danger of death? Each of these sacraments increases and strengthens our life of grace. *Confirmation, Holy Eucharist, Anointing of the Sick, Holy Orders, and Matrimony are called sacraments of the living because their chief purpose is to give more grace to souls already alive through grace.* How are these sacraments different from Baptism and Penance and Reconciliation? Recall the chief purpose of the sacraments of the dead.

Christ gave us two sacraments to use when our souls do not have the life of grace. Which two are they? He gave us five sacraments through which we can increase our life of grace. Which five are they? If we knowingly and deliberately receive one of these sacraments of the living while we are in the state of mortal sin, our act could be likened to taking the wrong kind of medicine. The sacrament does not help us; it harms us. We commit a mortal sin of sacrilege. *He who knowingly receives a sacrament of the living in mortal sin commits a mortal sin of sacrilege.* Which sacrament should we receive to have our sins forgiven and to have our life of grace restored?

Sacraments Which Can Be Received Only Once

Some of the sacraments can be received as often as we need them. For example, the more often and the more devoutly we go to confession and receive Holy Communion the more grace we receive. We may receive the sacrament of the Anointing of the Sick as often as it is necessary. A person may even receive Matrimony more than once if his partner in marriage dies. There are three sacraments which we did not mention: *Baptism, Confirmation, and Holy Orders can be received only once because they imprint on the soul a spiritual mark which lasts forever.* The spiritual mark is never lost, the soul bears this spiritual mark forever.

TERMS TO KNOW

- supernatural life
- sacraments of the dead
- immortal
- sacraments of the living
- sanctifying grace
- sacramental grace
- sacrilege
- life of grace
- actual grace
- spiritual mark

FOR ME TO STUDY

Catechism Lesson

136. Q. What is a sacrament?

A. A sacrament is an outward sign instituted by Christ to give grace.

137. Q. How many sacraments are there?

A. There are seven sacraments: Baptism, Confirmation, Holy Eucharist, Penance and Reconciliation, Anointing of the Sick, Holy Orders, and Matrimony.

139. Q. What grace do the sacraments give?

A. Some of the sacraments give sanctifying grace, and others increase it in our souls.

140. Q. Which are the sacraments that give sanctifying grace?

A. The sacraments that give sanctifying grace are Baptism and Penance and Reconciliation; and they are called sacraments of the dead.

147. Q. Do the sacraments always give grace?

A. The sacraments always give grace, if we receive them with the right dispositions.

- *What do we mean when we say that the sacraments give grace if we receive them properly?*
- *What does mortal sin do to the soul?*

141. Q. Why are Baptism and Penance and Reconciliation called sacraments of the dead?

A. Baptism and Penance and Reconciliation are called sacraments of the dead, because they take away sin, which is the death of the soul, and give grace, which is its life.

143. Q. Why are Confirmation, Holy Eucharist, Anointing of the Sick, Holy Orders, and Matrimony called sacraments of the living?

A. Confirmation, Holy Eucharist, Anointing of the Sick, Holy Orders, and Matrimony are called sacraments of the living, because those who receive them worthily are already living the life of grace.

144. Q. What sin does he commit who receives the sacraments of the living in mortal sin?

A. He who receives the sacraments of the living in mortal sin commits a sacrilege, which is a great sin, because it is an abuse of a sacred thing.

149. Q. Why can we not receive Baptism, Confirmation, and Holy Orders more than once?

A. We cannot receive Baptism, Confirmation, and Holy Orders more than once, because they imprint a character in the soul.

FOR ME TO REMEMBER

1. God gave me supernatural powers because He loves me and wants me to live with Him forever in heaven.
2. Sanctifying grace gives me supernatural life.
3. We receive grace through the merits of Jesus Christ.
4. The seven sacraments are a chief source of grace.
5. A sacrament is an outward sign instituted by Christ to give grace.
6. The sacraments of the dead are Baptism and Penance and Reconciliation.

7. The sacraments of the dead give the life of grace to the soul.
8. Confirmation, Holy Eucharist, Anointing of the Sick, Holy Orders, and Matrimony are sacraments of the living.
9. The sacraments of the living give more grace to souls already alive through grace.
10. The sacraments also give a special sacramental grace.
11. We commit a grave sin of sacrilege if we knowingly receive a sacrament of the living in mortal sin.
12. Baptism, Confirmation, and Holy Orders can be received only once.

FOR ME TO DO

1. Thank God for sending His Son to give us the wonderful gift of the sacraments.
2. Resolve to go to confession and receive Communion frequently.
3. Encourage others to go to confession—"Hey, Jimmy, let's go to confession together."
4. Arrange for the sick persons in my family and neighborhood to receive the Anointing of the Sick.

La pénitence. La penitencia.
La penitenza. Die Busse.
L'eucharistie. L'eucaristia.
L'eucarestia. Das heiligste Altarsacrament.
La confirmation. La confirmacion.
La cresima. Die Firmung.
Le baptême. El bautismo.
Il battesimo. Die Taufe.
L'extrême-onction. La extremauncion.
L'olio santo. Die letzte Oelung.
L'ordre. La ordenacion.
ordine sacro. Die Priesterweihe.
Le mariage. El matrimonio.
Il matrimonio. Die Ehe.

CHAPTER 17
Baptism

LESSON 33

A New Life of Grace

What Baptism Is

James was happy and excited because he was going to the Knights of Columbus' Father and Son Banquet. In addition to a wonderful turkey dinner with all the trimmings, there was going to be a movie of the Rose Bowl Football Game and prizes and presents for everybody. It was going to be really worthwhile! But the grandest feature of this party was that it would be free. That is, it was free for James because his father was a member of the Knights of Columbus.

When James' father joined the Knights he was given a membership card. This entitled him to all the rights and privileges of the club. On the night of the banquet, James' father would only have to show his membership card and James and his father would be admitted to an evening of fun. He was entitled to all this because his father was a member of the club.

Which sacrament can be compared with and is ever so much more valuable than the membership card of James' father? The sacrament of Baptism; it gives us the right to privileges far greater than those of any club. Baptism makes us members of Christ's true Church. It makes us His adopted brothers, for *Baptism is the sacrament that gives our souls the new life of grace by which we become children of God.* What is another name for the new life of grace? In your home you share in everything your mother and

father provide for the family because you are a member of the family. As children of God, we are members of His family and, therefore, share in everything God provides for His family. A godfather and a godmother are appointed the task of instructing the newly baptized in his religious duties. They are present during the baptism in order to promise, in the name of the child, what the child himself would promise if he had the use of reason.

What Baptism Does for Us

Besides giving us sanctifying grace, Baptism also takes something away from our soul, namely, original sin. You know the story of how we inherit original sin. If there is time, perhaps you may tell it to your class.

Usually Baptism is given to babies who are only a few days old. Would they have any sin on their souls besides original sin? Does it ever happen that older boys and girls, and even adults, are not baptized? Would they be guilty of actual sins? You remember that an actual sin is one that we ourselves commit. In such cases *Baptism takes away original sin; and also actual sins, if there be any, and all punishment due to them.* God is very good to us!

When Sister Mary Catherine was checking on the boys and girls who came for religious instructions on Monday after school hours, because they attended a public school, she found that there were two boys who had never been baptized. They were about ten years old and were very anxious to be baptized and receive their first Holy Communion. After the boys had been given sufficient instruction, Father set the date and made arrangements to baptize them. Were these boys probably guilty of any actual sins? Would such sins be forgiven when the boys were baptized? What else did Baptism free them of? Did you ever watch a Baptism? Where do Baptisms take place in Church?

Who May Baptize

Jesus Christ gave the Apostles the power to baptize. He said to them: "Go, therefore, and make disciples of all nations, baptizing them in the name of the Father and of the Son and of the Holy Spirit" (Mt. 29:19–20). This same power to baptize is passed on to the priests in the Church. *The priest is the usual minister of Baptism, but if there is danger that someone will die without Baptism, any one else may and should baptize.* We must remember that Holy Mother Church is anxious to help all human beings to reach the goal for which God created them. Recall why God made us. Remember, too, what Christ told Nicodemus when he came seeking knowledge about God and eternal salvation. Christ said: "Amen, Amen, I say to thee unless a man be born again of water and the Holy Spirit, he cannot enter into the kingdom of God" (Jn. 3:5–6).

Because Christ desires that all be baptized, the Church not only gives her permission but urges anyone to baptize if there is danger that someone will die without the sacrament of Baptism. A nurse, for instance, could baptize a baby who is in danger of death, if there is no priest near. In such a case the nurse should baptize the baby. Would you be allowed to baptize the boy or girl next door to you just because you thought they should be baptized? Why not? Because those with the use of reason cannot be baptized unless they wish to receive Baptism and are properly instructed.

How Baptism Is Given

When the priest gives the sacrament of Baptism, he uses holy water and performs the ceremony according to the ritual of the Church. This includes many beautiful prayers and meaningful sacred actions. But let us suppose that it is necessary for me to give Baptism. How would I do it? *I would give Baptism by pouring ordinary water on the forehead of the person to be baptized, saying while pouring it: "I baptize thee in the name of the Father, and of the Son, and of the Holy Spirit."* Remember, you must say the words and pour the water at the same time. Can you think of any time when you would find it necessary to baptize someone?

FOR ME TO STUDY

Catechism Lesson

152. Q. What is Baptism?

A. Baptism is sacrament which cleanses us from original sin, makes us Christians, children of God, and heirs of heaven.

- *Explain what is meant when we say that Baptism makes us children of God.*

153. Q. Are actual sins ever remitted by Baptism?

A. Actual sins and all the punishment due to them are remitted by Baptism, if the person baptized be guilty of any.

- *Give an example in which Baptism would take away actual sin.*

155. Q. Who can administer Baptism?

A. The priest is the ordinary minister of Baptism; but in case of necessity any one who has the use of reason may baptize.

- *When may anyone besides the priest baptize?*
- *What did Christ tell Nicodemus when he came seeking knowledge about God and eternal salvation?*

156. Q. How is Baptism given?

A. Whoever baptizes should pour water on the head of the person to be baptized, and say, while pouring the water: "I baptize thee in the name of the Father, and of the Son, and of the Holy Spirit."

164. Q. Why are godfathers and godmothers given in Baptism?

A. Godfathers and godmothers are given in Baptism in order that they may promise, in the name of the child, what the child itself would promise if it had the use of reason.

165. Q. **What is the obligation of a godfather and a godmother?**

A. The obligation of a godfather and a godmother is to instruct the child in its religious duties, if the parents neglect to do so or die.

FOR ME TO REMEMBER

1. Baptism is the sacrament that gives our souls the new life of grace by which we become children of God.
2. In certain cases it takes away actual sins and all punishment due to them.
3. Baptism takes away original sin.
4. The priest is the usual minister of Baptism.
5. If it is necessary for me to baptize, remember to pour ordinary water on the forehead of the person to be baptized and say while pouring it: "I baptize thee in the name of the Father, and of the Son, and of the Holy Spirit."
6. Adults must want to be baptized and be instructed.

FOR ME TO DO

1. Learn the date of my Baptism. Celebrate my "Spiritual birthday" by going to Mass and receiving Holy Communion in thanksgiving for the gift of Baptism.
2. In my own words, say a prayer of thanksgiving to Christ for giving me the gift of Baptism.
3. I will think of my Baptism every time I bless myself with holy water and thank God for that great grace.

CHAPTER 18
Confirmation

LESSON 34

What Confirmation Is

After Christ ascended into heaven, the Apostles returned to Jerusalem. There they remained together in one place waiting for the Holy Spirit who had been promised by Christ. St. Luke tells what happened in the Acts of the Apostles. "And suddenly there came a sound from heaven, as of a violent wind coming, and it filled the whole house where they were sitting. And there appeared to them parted tongues as of fire, which settled upon each of them. And they were all filled with the Holy Spirit and began to speak in foreign tongues, even as the Holy Spirit prompted them to speak" (Acts 2:2–4).

The Apostles were strengthened in their faith. Fearlessly they began to preach the Gospel of Christ. The Holy Spirit strengthened them in the Christian life of virtue and grace, ready and willing to work bravely for God, and even to die as martyrs. How do we become strong Christians? It is true that we received the Holy Spirit when we were baptized. At that time we received the supernatural life for the first time, but that life must grow and become strong. In a natural way we grow from children to adults. So too, our spiritual life must grow and become strong. In His wisdom Christ provided for our need by instituting the sacrament of Confirmation. *Confirmation is the sacrament through which the Holy Spirit comes to us in a special way and enables us to profess our faith as strong and perfect Christians and soldiers of Jesus Christ.*

Soldiers of Jesus Christ

As Catholic boys and girls, we know that our true home is the Kingdom of Heaven of which almighty God is the Divine Ruler. Our government provides an army whose duty it is to protect our country. Almighty God wills that His children work and live in the interest of His heavenly Kingdom, just as soldiers serve their country. Jesus Christ is the Leader of God's soldiers. Do you know who His soldiers are? The title of this chapter tells us if we do not already know. Those who receive the sacrament of Confirmation become soldiers of Jesus Christ.

In this sacrament the Holy Spirit increases and strengthens the three great virtues which we received at Baptism. (Can you name them?) The seven gifts of the Holy Spirit (Do you remember them, too?) are also going to be developed and perfected, because we are about to do battle with the enemies of God and His Church. We shall have to profess our faith, that is, show openly by our actions that we believe in God, that we are His soldiers. The gifts of the Holy Spirit will help us to do this.

You know how large a baseball park or stadium is. You know, too, how crowded it is for an important game or a doubleheader. That is the setting for this story. Michael was attending a game with his uncle. Between the first and second inning Michael decided to treat his uncle and himself to a delicious hot dog. His uncle did not notice Michael buying the hot dogs. When Michael offered him one, his uncle told him it was Friday. Do you know what Michael did? He turned to his neighbor and said, "I just bought these two 'hot dogs.' I forgot it's Friday.

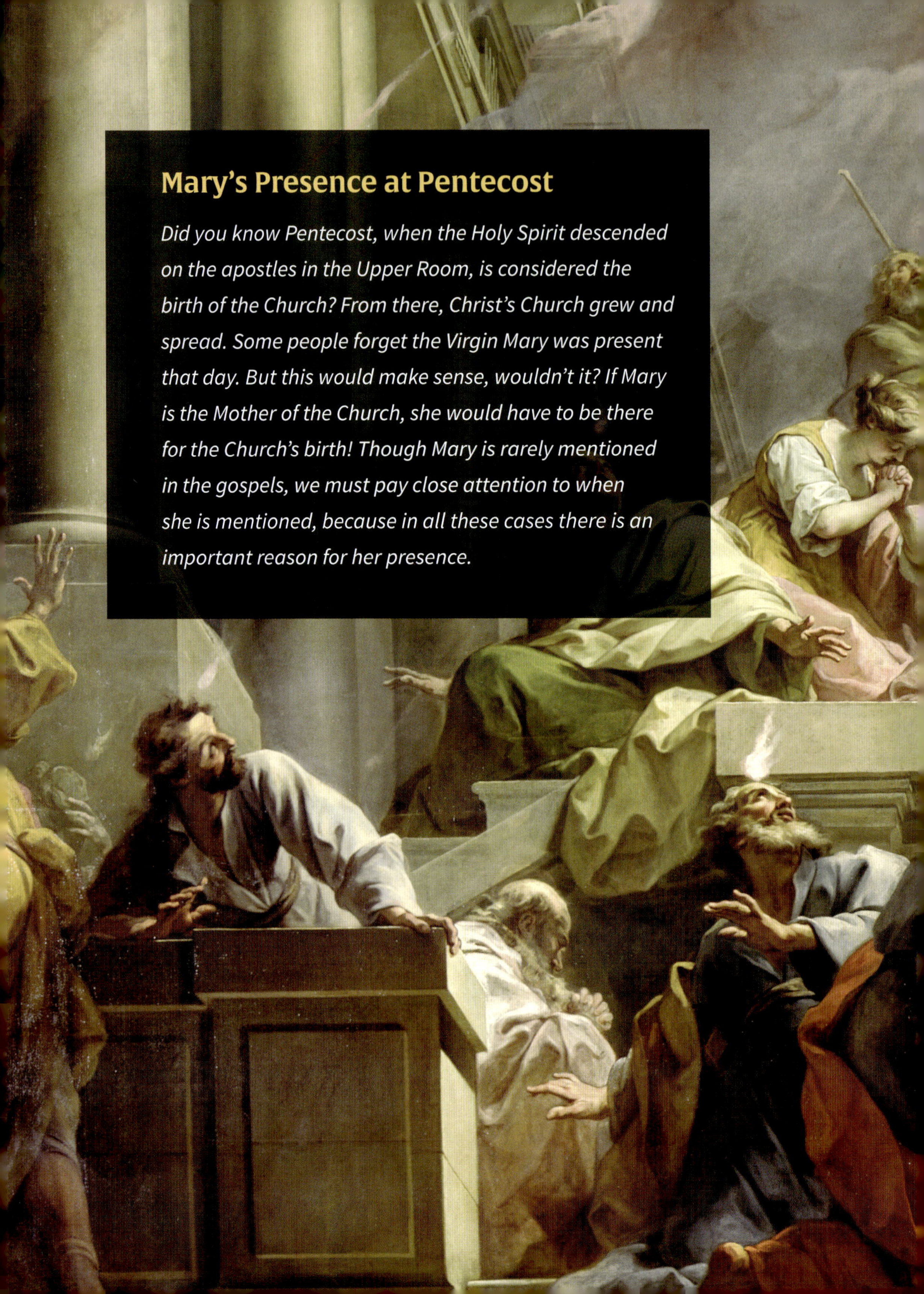

Mary's Presence at Pentecost

Did you know Pentecost, when the Holy Spirit descended on the apostles in the Upper Room, is considered the birth of the Church? From there, Christ's Church grew and spread. Some people forget the Virgin Mary was present that day. But this would make sense, wouldn't it? If Mary is the Mother of the Church, she would have to be there for the Church's birth! Though Mary is rarely mentioned in the gospels, we must pay close attention to when she is mentioned, because in all these cases there is an important reason for her presence.

Do you want them?" You may be sure he did. Did Michael profess his faith? Do you think it was easy? Has anything like this ever happened to you?

After boys and girls are confirmed, they must begin at once to show that they are Christ's soldiers in their everyday life. For instance, they must be brave enough to refuse meat sandwiches on Friday when some of their companions are enjoying them. Boys who go to camp with non-Catholics during the summer vacation must have courage to attend Sunday Mass and say prayers even if the others make fun of them. Girls can prove that they are Christ's soldiers by being modest in their dress and behavior when others around them are displeasing God by immodest fashions or behavior.

Who May Confirm

The Bishop is the usual minister of Confirmation. In confirming, the Bishop anoints the forehead with holy chrism. We say the Bishop is the "usual minister" of Confirmation because ordinarily the Bishop is the one who gives this sacrament. However, a priest can be given the authority and the power by the Pope to administer the sacrament of Confirmation if it is necessary. The Pope has often granted these powers to missionary priests.

In recent years Pope Pius XII gave pastors and certain other priests the authority and power to confirm persons who are in danger of death.

All Catholics should be confirmed in order to be strengthened against the dangers to salvation and to be prepared better to defend their Catholic faith. What would you think of a soldier who went into battle without weapons? Would he be of any assistance to his army? The sacrament of Confirmation provides us with a means of self-defense against the dangers to our supernatural life. Catholics who are confirmed are not only better able to save their own souls, but they are aided in defending their faith.

"Be sealed with the gift of the Holy Spirit"

FOR ME TO STUDY

Catechism Lesson

166. Q. What is Confirmation?

A. Confirmation is a sacrament through which we receive the Holy Spirit to make us strong and perfect Christians and soldiers of Jesus Christ.

Explain what is meant when we say the Holy Spirit comes to us in a special way in Confirmation.

Explain the meaning of the phrase: "to profess our faith."

167. Q. Who administers Confirmation?

A. The Bishop is the ordinary minister of Confirmation.

When may a priest give the sacrament of Confirmation?

Use these phrases in sentences:

- profess our faith
- usual minister of Confirmation

FOR ME TO REMEMBER

1. The Holy Spirit comes to us in a special way in the sacrament of Confirmation.

2. When we are confirmed, the Holy Spirit increases and strengthens the gifts He gave us at Baptism.

3. Confirmation is the sacrament through which the Holy Spirit comes to us in a special way to enable us to profess our faith as strong and perfect Christians and soldiers of Jesus Christ.

4. The bishop is the usual minister of Confirmation.

5. A priest may be given the power and authority to confirm in case of necessity.

6. All Catholics should be confirmed in order to be strengthened against the dangers to salvation and to be prepared better to defend their Catholic faith.

FOR ME TO DO

Learn and recite the prayer *Come Holy Spirit* every day.

Come Holy Spirit

Come, Holy Spirit, fill the hearts of Thy faithful and enkindle in them the fire of Thy love. Send forth Thy Spirit and they shall be created. And Thou shalt renew the face of the earth.

Let us pray:

O God, who didst instruct the hearts of the faithful by the light of the Holy Spirit, grant us in the same Spirit to be truly wise, and ever to rejoice in His consolation. Through Christ our Lord. Amen.

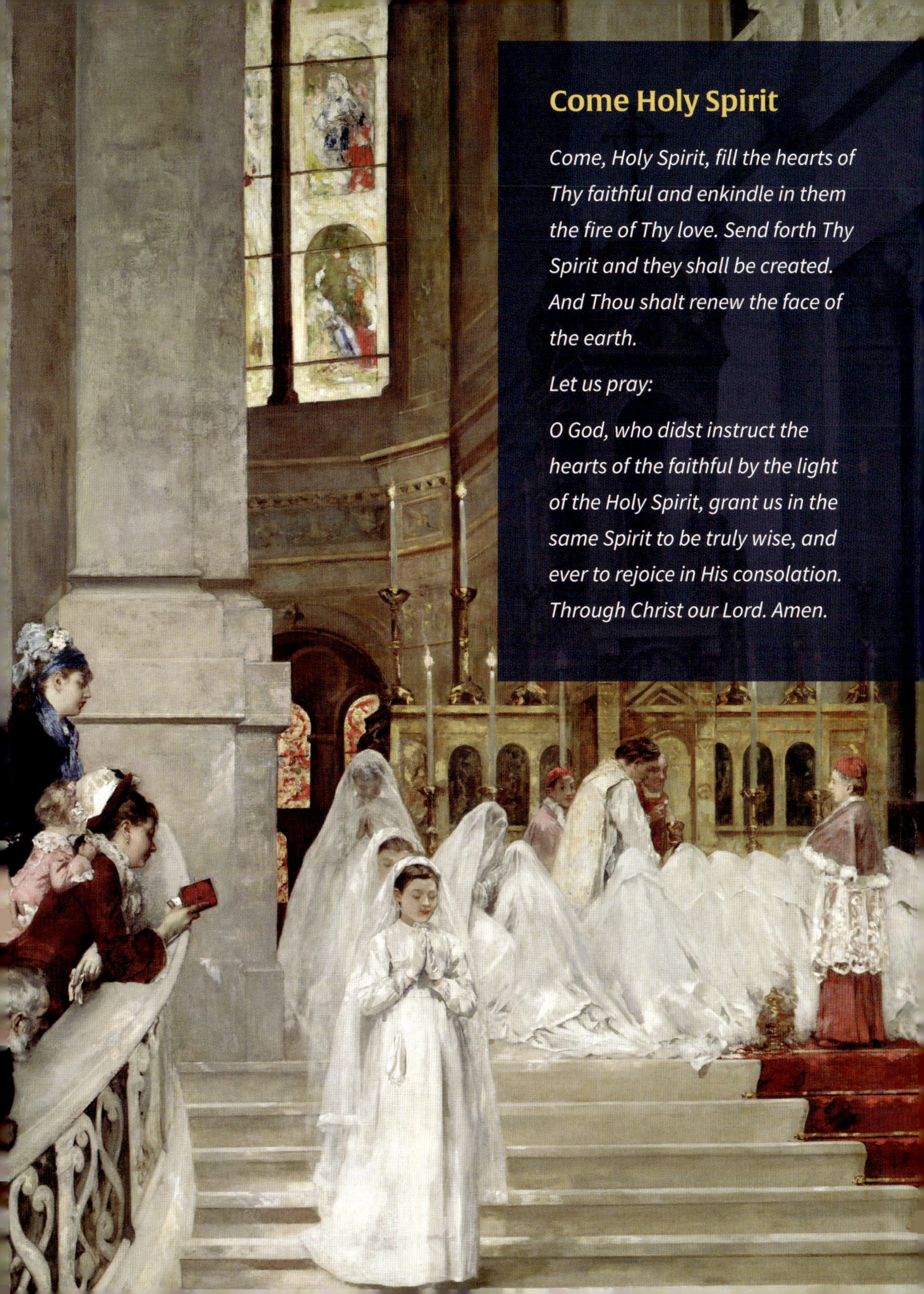

CHAPTER 19
The Holy Eucharist

LESSON 35

The Bread of Life

Christ Fulfills His Promise to His Apostles

While He sat at supper with His Apostles on Holy Thursday, Jesus Christ knew that on the following day He would be condemned to death. As always, Christ thought not of Himself nor of His suffering but of His chosen friends. He wanted to give them a remembrance of Him that they would keep for all time. What wonderful gift had He planned to give to them? His very own Self; He willed to give His Body, Blood, Soul, and Divinity, as a Victim to be offered to God to adore Him, as well as to atone for men's sins, and to be the Food of their souls.

How could our Lord give them Himself? He did it by giving them the Holy Eucharist. *The Holy Eucharist is a sacrament and a sacrifice. In the Holy Eucharist, under the appearances of bread and wine the Lord Christ is contained, offered, and received.*

Christ instituted the Holy Eucharist at the Last Supper, the night before He died. He took bread, blessed and broke it giving it to His Apostles, and said: "Take and eat, this is My body." Then He took a cup of wine, blessed it and giving it to them, and said: "All of you drink of this, for this is My blood of the new covenant, which is being shed for many unto the forgiveness of sins" (Mt. 26:27–28).

When our Lord said, "This is My body," the bread was changed into His body, and when He said, "This is My blood," the wine was changed into His blood. After the bread and wine had been

changed into our Lord's body and blood, there remained only the appearances of bread and wine. By appearances of bread and wine we mean their color, taste, weight, and shape, and whatever else appears to the senses.

Christ Fulfills His Promise to All Mankind

Only the Apostles were with Christ when He instituted the Blessed Sacrament. Were they to receive this great gift only this one time and never again? Were they to be the only ones ever to receive the precious Body and Blood of Christ? No, as you already know our Lord thought of us and He wanted to give Himself to us, too. He wanted to give Himself as the Food for all men. What did our Lord do to make this possible? He gave the same power to His priests. When? *Christ gave His priests the power to change bread and wine into His body and blood when He said to the Apostles at the Last Supper: "Do this in remembrance of Me."* The Apostles passed this power to other priests so that today we receive Christ Himself just the same as the Apostles did on that first Holy Thursday night.

TERMS TO KNOW

- contained
- offered
- power
- received
- appearances

FOR ME TO STUDY

Catechism Lesson

238. Q. What is the Holy Eucharist?

A. The Holy Eucharist is the sacrament which contains the Body and Blood, Soul and Divinity, of our Lord Jesus Christ under the appearances of bread and wine.

239. Q. When did Christ institute the Holy Eucharist?

A. Christ instituted the Holy Eucharist at the Last Supper, the night before He died.

241. Q. How did our Lord institute the Holy Eucharist?

A. Our Lord instituted the Holy Eucharist by taking bread, blessing, breaking, and giving to His Apostles, saying: "Take ye and eat, This is My body"; and then by taking the cup of wine, blessing and giving it, saying to them: "Drink ye all of this. This is My blood which shall be shed for the remission of sins. Do this in remembrance of Me."

244. Q. Did anything remain of the bread and wine after their substance had been changed into the substance of the body and blood of our Lord?

A. After the substance of the bread and wine had been changed into the substance of the body and blood of our Lord there remained only the appearances of bread and wine.

245. Q. What do you mean by the appearances of bread and wine?

A. By the appearances of bread and wine I mean the figure, the color, the taste, and whatever appears to the senses.

- *Who was with our Lord at the Last Supper?*
- *How did Christ give the Apostles the power to change bread and wine into His body and blood?*

249. **Q. When did Christ give His priests the power to change bread and wine into His body and blood?**

A. Christ gave His priests the power to change bread and wine into His body and blood when He said to the Apostles, "Do this in remembrance of Me."

FOR ME TO REMEMBER

1. The Holy Eucharist is a sacrament and a sacrifice.
2. Christ instituted the Holy Eucharist at the Last Supper on Holy Thursday night.
3. After the bread and wine are changed into the body and blood of Christ, the appearances remain the same.
4. Christ gave His Apostles the power to change bread and wine into His body and blood at the Last Supper when He said, "Do this in remembrance of Me."

FOR ME TO DO

1. If we cannot receive Christ under the appearances of bread and wine every day, we can make a spiritual communion as often as we wish by saying, My dear Jesus, I love You. Come into my heart and stay with me always.
2. Make up my own spiritual communion prayer and recite it during this day.
3. Visit Christ often in the tabernacle.

The Sacraments: Baptism, Confirmation, Holy Eucharist

Write your answers on a separate sheet of paper

PART 1 *Matching*

Match the beginnings and endings of the following sentences:

A. Beginnings	**B. Endings**
1. The sacraments give	A. instituted by Christ to give grace.
2. Each sacrament gives a special grace	B. to receive the other sacraments.
3. The sacrament is an outward sign	C. sanctifying grace if we receive them properly.
4. The sacraments have the power of giving grace	D. sacraments of the dead.
5. Baptism makes us	E. members of the Church and children of God.
6. If there is danger that a baby will die without Baptism	F. because of the merits of Christ.
7. Baptism makes it possible	G. anyone may and should baptize him.
8. Baptism and Penance and Reconciliation are called	H. called sacramental grace.

PART II *Completion*

Complete the following sentences by supplying the missing words:

1. Sacraments that can be received more than once are (1), (2), (3), and (4).
2. One who receives the sacraments of the living in mortal sin commits (5).
3. The sacraments (6), (7), and (8) can be received only once.
4. The sin which we inherit from Adam and Eve is (9).
5. The usual minister of Baptism is (10).
6. The sacraments of (11) give supernatural life of grace to souls spiritually dead through sin.
7. A name of a (12) is given at Baptism so that we may imitate his life and have him for a protector.
8. The most necessary sacrament is (13).
9. (14) grace gives us supernatural life.
10. If I were called upon in an emergency to baptize a dying baby, I would do the following (15).
11. Mary's little brother Daniel was baptized last week. List the changes that took place in Daniel when he was baptized (16).
12. Write the words of Christ to Nicodemus that show that Baptism is necessary for salvation (17).

PART III. *Yes or No.*

Answer the following questions with Yes or No.

1. Is Confirmation a sacrament of the dead?
2. Does the sacrament of Confirmation make us soldiers of Jesus Christ?
3. May we receive the sacrament of Confirmation more than once?
4. Is the bishop the usual minister of Confirmation?
5. Does the Holy Spirit come to us in a special way through Confirmation?
6. Does Confirmation strengthen us against dangers to salvation?
7. Should all Catholics be confirmed?
8. Does Confirmation prepare us to defend our faith?
9. May a priest ever give the sacrament of Confirmation?
10. Does the Holy Spirit give us the theological virtues in Confirmation?

PART IV *Completion*

Complete the following sentences by supplying the missing words:

1. Confirmation is a sacrament through which we receive the Holy Spirit to make us strong and perfect (1) and (2) of Jesus Christ.
2. The (3) is the usual minister of Confirmation.
3. Christ instituted the Holy Eucharist at the (4).
4. The Holy Eucharist is a sacrament and a sacrifice; in it our Saviour, Jesus Christ, body and blood, soul and divinity, under the appearances of bread and wine is (5), (6), and (7).
5. By the appearances of bread and wine we mean their (8), (9), (10), and (11) and whatever else appears to the senses.
6. When our Lord said, "This is My body," the (12) was changed into His body; and when He said, "This is my blood," the (13) was changed into His blood.

CHAPTER 20
Holy Mass: The Perfect Sacrifice

LESSON 36

Sacrifice, An Act of Worship

From the beginning of time men have recognized God as their almighty Creator from whom they have received all things. They wished to adore and love Him and so they offered sacrifices to Him. That is what Abel and Noah and Abraham did, too. They offered sacrifice to God to show that they loved Him and recognized Him as the Creator of heaven and earth and of all things.

When they offered sacrifice they gave God something they had and which they loved very much. Here we shall learn a new and deeper meaning of the word sacrifice. In a true sacrifice a victim is offered to God and a priest offers it. Abraham as well as others in the Old Testament often offered a lamb as the victim. They placed it upon an altar, and the priest slaughtered and burned the victim, after he had offered it to God.

What was the meaning of such a sacrifice? The people were adoring God by offering a lamb in sacrifice. God loved their sacrifices because He knew that the gifts were signs of their love and their sorrow for sin. God loved their sacrifices, too, because He knew the lambs that were offered represented the very lives of those who were offering the sacrifice. The people were saying to God, as it were: "God, You are worthy that I offer my own life to You as a victim of sacrifice. But I am not allowed to take my life. So let this victim take my place to show how much I adore and

thank and love You, how sorry I am for my sins, and how much I need Your grace to avoid sin in the future."

Jesus Christ Offers the Perfect Bloody Sacrifice

Most of these sacrifices were pleasing to God. He knew that the hearts of those who offered the sacrifices were good; He knew that the victims, which were offered in the sacrifices, were the best that man could afford.

TERMS TO KNOW

- sacrifice
- priest
- victim
- perfect bloody sacrifice
- perfect unbloody sacrifice

Yet, these sacrifices did not satisfy almighty God entirely, because neither the priests who offered the sacrifices nor the victims of the sacrifices were perfect. In our study of the Creed, we learned that only One is truly perfect, God Himself. It was necessary for God to become man before a perfect sacrifice could be offered. Only such a sacrifice could atone for man's sin. Christ became the perfect priest, and because He offered Himself, He offered His heavenly Father a perfect victim. Just as in the Old Testament the victim of the sacrifice had to be offered and consumed, so Christ in the New Testament offered Himself and gave up His life for us. On the cross Christ really shed His blood and was really slain. His suffering and death on the cross were the perfect bloody sacrifice which truly satisfied almighty God for sin and reopened the gates of heaven.

Jesus Christ Offers the Perfect Unbloody Sacrifice

At the Last Supper Christ took bread and said to the Apostles, "Take ye and eat, this is My body." Then he took wine and said, "Take ye and drink, this is My blood." Here again Christ was offering Himself, this time under the appearances of bread and wine. What else did Christ say to His Apostles at the Last Supper? He told them that they, too, should offer His body and blood under the appearances of bread and wine in remembrance of Him. "Do this in memory of me." The Apostles obeyed this command and passed it on to other priests. Each day, and at every minute of the day, Christ is being offered in the Holy Sacrifice of the Mass.

This sacrifice of the New Law is the same sacrifice as that offered by Christ at the Last Supper. It is the same sacrifice as the sacrifice of the cross. In each Mass Christ is the perfect priest and the perfect victim. *Mass is the same sacrifice as the sacrifice of the cross.*

However, *the manner in which the sacrifice is offered is different. On the cross Christ physically shed His blood and was physically slain, while in the Mass there is no physical shedding of blood nor physical death.* In the Mass Christ does not actually suffer; He does not shed His blood; He does not die again. The Mass is the re-enactment of the perfect bloody sacrifice in an unbloody manner. As the catechism says: *The Mass is the sacrifice of the New Law in which Christ, through the priest, offers Himself to God in an unbloody manner under the appearances of bread and wine.*

The Meaning of Re-Presentation

Some people incorrectly think Catholics re-sacrifice Jesus at each Mass. The word "re-presentation" helps us understand the truth. This word means "to make present again." We are not re-sacrificing Christ, but are making his once and for all sacrifice present again.

FOR ME TO STUDY

Catechism Lesson

263. Q. What is the Mass?

A. The Mass is the unbloody sacrifice of the body and blood of Christ.

265. Q. Is the Mass the samesacrifice as that of the cross?

A. The Mass is the same sacrifice as that of the cross.

268. Q. Is there any difference between the sacrifice of the cross and the sacrifice of the Mass?

A. Yes; the manner in which the sacrifice is offered is different. On the cross Christ really shed His blood and was really slain; in the Mass there is no real shedding of blood nor real death, because Christ can die no more; but the sacrifice of the Mass, through the separate consecration of the bread and the wine, represents His death on the cross.

FOR ME TO REMEMBER

1. A sacrifice is an act of worship in which a priest offers to God a victim for the purpose of showing love for Him and recognition of Him as the Creator of heaven and earth and all things.
2. The priest of the sacrifice is the one who offers the sacrifice.
3. The victim of the sacrifice is the thing which is offered.
4. The sacrifices of the Old Testament were, in general, pleasing to God but did not satisfy Him entirely because neither the priests nor the victims were perfect.

5. Jesus Christ offered God the perfect sacrifice because He Himself was the perfect priest and perfect victim.
6. Christ's suffering and death on the cross was the perfect bloody sacrifice.
7. When Christ offered His body and blood under the appearances of bread and wine, He offered the perfect unbloody sacrifice.
8. The sacrifice of Christ at the Last Supper is the same as the sacrifice of the Mass and the sacrifice of Christ on the cross.
9. The sacrifice of the cross is re-enacted in an unbloody manner every day in the sacrifice of the Mass.
10. The Mass is the sacrifice of the New Law in which Christ, through the priest, offers Himself to God in an unbloody manner under the appearances of bread and wine.

FOR ME TO DO

I have studied about the great sacrifice which Christ offers to God for me. What sacrifice can I make for Him today? Make my wishes the same as His wishes? Offer my will to Him? Make some little sacrifice for Him? Give up my favorite comic strip or TV program? Give spending money for the missions? Give up a candy bar? A soft drink?

LESSON 37

The Mass, A Source of Grace

Christ once said: "I am the vine; you are the branches. He who abides in me, and I in him, he bears much fruit; for without me you can do nothing" (Jn. 15:5–6). Have you heard this quotation before? It is taken from a parable which Christ once told to His disciples. A parable is a story which Christ used as a way of teaching His followers about God and Himself. What do you think Christ was trying to teach us when He compared Himself to a vine and His disciples to the branches of that vine? Perhaps this example will help you to understand it more clearly.

Have you ever examined grapes when they were still growing on the vine? For one thing you probably noticed that the vine wound in and out so that you could hardly tell where it began or ended. You found that the bunches of grapes were held on strong stems which were attached to a heavy branch. This branch was growing from another. As you looked more closely you saw that all the branches were connected with one big, strong, main stem. If you traced this central stem, you learned that it was coming from roots hidden deep down in the ground. These roots were supplying the vine with nourishment, which in turn was carried out to the branches, the leaves, and the grapes. What would happen to any branch if it were cut or broken off from the vine? Would it bear leaves? Would it produce grapes? No, it would be unable to get food, and soon it would wither and die.

When Christ says that He is the vine and we are the branches, He is telling us that we, too, receive our life and our strength and nourishment from Him. This life, strength, and nourishment comes to us as grace, without which we can do nothing.

Your entire fourth grade religion study centered on the sacred liturgy through which we receive grace and are united with Christ. Your chief aim was to learn to live the life which is contained and is taught in the liturgy and in the Church year. The Mass is the center of the liturgy. It is the highest form of worship. It is a sacrifice through which we adore God's greatness and through which we in turn receive graces of infinite value. Through the Holy Sacrifice of the Mass, we are united with Christ in a way in which no other prayer or form of worship can unite us to Him.

At the Last Supper, when Christ first offered His body and blood, He gave His Apostles this sacrifice. The Apostles were directed to change bread and wine into the Body and Blood of Christ. Yet, when we assist at Mass, we hear and see much more than just this one action performed by the priest. Who introduced the other actions and prayers which are included in our Mass today?

Think back to our study of the precepts of the Church. Did we not learn that the Church has the power and the right to make any changes which she considers helpful or necessary? The Church used this power and this right in order to help us show the proper reverence for the tremendous Sacrifice of the Mass. She knew that the act of changing bread and wine into the body and blood of Christ should be surrounded by other actions and prayers. That is why the Church has added ceremonies and prayers, some in preparation and others in thanksgiving for the great gift of God Himself to man.

Before any important event, or before carrying out any great activity, you make the proper preparation. Think of the important feasts like Christmas, Easter, and all the holy days of obligation. What great preparations are made so that the feasts can be observed as the Church wishes them to be! So, too, with the Mass. There must be time for proper preparation, for the Mass is the great act of the liturgy.

We Prepare

This is the title we give to the first part of the Mass. We prepare in two ways: first, by praying, and second by listening and learning. We watch the priest as he walks into the sanctuary. He stops before the altar, genuflects, and then goes up the steps. There he stops and kisses the altar stone which contains the relics of the saints. The priest then goes to the missal and reads the *Introit,* or *Entrance Antiphon*, if it was not recited or sung during the procession. This prayer expresses the main thought of the feast or of the season in which the feast occurs. The feast may recall a joyous event or one of sorrow, it may remind us to do penance, or it may be one giving us a feeling of hope. Because the *Introit* changes from day to day, it is a part of the *Proper of the Mass*. Those prayers which are the same for every Mass are called the *Ordinary of the Mass.*

We Pray—We Speak to God

We join the priest as he makes the *Sign of the Cross*. You have already observed the cross on the altar; you also have seen it on the priest's vestments. Now he makes the Sign of the Cross on himself as the first prayer of the Mass. The frequent use of the cross helps us to realize that we are about to see the mystery of the cross re-enacted once more. It also serves as an act of faith in the Trinity. This Sign of the Cross is also an act by which we tell God that we give Him our mind in faith, as we place our fingers on our foreheads; our hearts in love, as we place our fingers on our breasts; our entire self, as we place our fingers first on our left shoulders and then on our right.

Following the Sign of the Cross, *the Confiteor* is then recited by the priest and by all the faithful present at Mass. In the Confiteor we acknowledge our offenses against God, express our sorrow, and ask pardon and forgiveness in the presence of the great saints of heaven. The Confiteor is something like another prayer that you recite every time you go to confession. What is the name of that prayer? How is the Act of Contrition like the Confiteor? Can you say both prayers?

TERMS TO KNOW

- Introit
- Proper of the Mass
- Ordinary of the Mass
- Sign of the Cross
- Confiteor
- Kyrie Eleison
- Gloria in Excelsis Deo
- Collect

We then recite the *Kyrie Eleison.* This prayer is a plea for mercy. In some Masses the priest and the faithful present next recite the *Gloria in Excelsis Deo.* Have you ever heard these words before? Who first said them and what was the occasion?

Just as the angels sang these words on the first Christmas night to give praise and glory to almighty God, so the priest in the Mass repeats them for the same purpose. He, too, wishes to give glory to God the Father, the Son, and the Holy Spirit. The Gloria is omitted during the seasons of Advent and Lent. It is never said during a Requiem Mass, that is, a Mass which is offered for the soul of a person who has died.

Throughout the Mass, the priest turns to the people and says, "Dominus Vobiscum." This greeting, "The Lord be with you," is heard often during the Mass. The people respond, "et cum spiritu tuo," that is, "and with your spirit."

The priest returns to the missal and reads the *Collect*. This prayer, like the Introit, changes according to the feast of the day. What did we say was the name given to the parts of the Mass that change from day to day? The Collect is one of these prayers, belonging to the Proper of the Mass. In some Masses the priest says more than one Collect. The Collect brings together in one the many prayers of the priest and the people who are collected for the Mass. They ask God for help for both body and soul.

FOR ME TO REMEMBER

1. The Mass is the source of infinite graces.
2. The Church has added ceremonies and prayers to the Mass.
3. The Sign of the Cross is the first action to be performed in the Mass.
4. In the Confiteor we acknowledge our offenses against God, express our sorrow, and ask pardon and forgiveness.
5. The priest kisses the altar to reverence the relics of the saints.
6. The Introit expresses the spirit of the feast.
7. Prayers which do not change from day to day are known as the Ordinary of the Mass.
8. Prayers which change from day to day are known as the Proper of the Mass.
9. The Kyrie Eleison is a plea for mercy in honor of God the Father, Son, and Holy Spirit.
10. The Gloria is a hymn of praise.
11. The Collect gathers together the prayer of the priest and the people collected for the Mass.

FOR ME TO STUDY

1. What does Christ wish us to learn from His parable of the vine and the branches?
2. Explain why the Mass today includes more actions and prayers than did the first Mass offered by Christ at the Last Supper.
3. In what two ways do we prepare for the sacrifice of the Mass?
4. Why do we begin Mass with the Sign of the Cross?
5. Why is the Confiteor an important preparatory prayer?
6. Explain the use of relics on the altar.
7. What is the Introit?
8. Explain what is meant by the Proper of the Mass; the Ordinary of the Mass.
9. Is the Gloria sung in all Masses?
10. What is the Collect?
11. Do you know these terms? Match each term in Column I with its meaning in Column II:

Column I	Column II
A. Parable	1. Mass for the dead
B. Confiteor	2. The Lord be with you
C. Gloria in Excelsis Deo	3. A story used by Christ to teach a lesson.
D. Dominus vobiscum	4. Prayers which change from day to day
E. Collect	5. Prayer in which we confess our sins
F. Proper of the Mass	6. Hymn of praise sung first by the angels.
G. Ordinary of the Mass	7. Prayers which are the same in every Mass.
H. Introit	8. A prayer in the name of those collected for the Mass.
I. Kyrie Eleison	9. A plea for mercy
J. Requiem Mass	10. A prayer keynoting the spirit of the feast.

FOR ME TO DO

1. Learn the Confiteor and say it with the priest when he says it during Mass.
2. Read the Gloria prayer slowly and thoughtfully.
3. Join in the words and actions of the Mass with great reverence.

LESSON 38

We Learn—God Speaks to Us

The Apostles, you remember, were told to go out and teach the word of God to everyone. They were not able to remain in one place all the time. They had to go out into all parts of the world.

What would happen to us if we had no priests to help us know God? We would not be able to receive the sacraments, we would not be able to assist at Mass, and there would come a time when people would not even know God. The Apostles knew this would happen to the early Christians, too. Therefore, because they could not stay with the people, they wrote letters of instruction which the people could read from time to time. These letters were called Epistles.

On Sunday there are three readings during Mass. The first is from the Old Testament, the second is from the New Testament (usually from one of the Epistles), and the third reading is taken from one of the four Gospel accounts.

Every Sunday you hear the Gospel read aloud. Do you recall what it was about last Sunday? Have you ever noticed that it is always about something Christ did or said? The Gospel is a portion of the life of Christ. The account of Christ's life was written

The Gloria

Glory to God in the highest, and on earth peace to people of good will. We praise you, we bless you, we adore you, we glorify you, we give you thanks for your great glory, Lord God, heavenly King, O God almighty Father.

Lord Jesus Christ, Only Begotten Son, Lord God, Lamb of God, Son of the Father, you take away the sins of the world, have mercy on us; you take away the sins of the world, receive our prayer; you are seated at the right hand of the Father, have mercy on us.

For You alone are the Holy One, you alone are the Lord, you alone are the Most High, Jesus Christ, with the Holy Spirit, in the glory of God the Father. Amen.

St. Anthony of Padua

St. Anthony was present once on the occasion of a very important celebration. Many bishops and other high dignitaries of the Church were assembled for Mass. As the Mass progressed it was discovered that no one had been appointed to preach the sermon. No one wanted to volunteer, for who would feel capable of preaching on such an occasion with no preparation. St. Anthony was then summoned by his superior and directed to pray for enlightenment and then preach whatever the Holy Spirit put into his mind. St. Anthony obeyed. His first words came slowly and timidly. Soon he was preaching with great ease, holding the attention of all who were present.

St. Anthony knew that the Holy Spirit was helping him. After Mass, St. Anthony was praised for his fine sermon. St. Anthony received the compliments graciously and said, "It was not I who spoke to you, but the Holy Spirit who spoke to you through me."

by the four evangelists, St. Matthew, St. Mark, St. Luke, and St. John. That is why you hear the priest announce the Gospel of St. John or the Gospel of St. Luke or some other evangelist. Each of these men wrote the life of Christ as God inspired him to write. So, when you listen to the Gospel you are hearing the very words of God Himself.

Does that explain why the priest makes a special preparation before he reads the Gospel? He shows great respect for the words of Christ. What do we do during the Gospel to show our reverence for Christ's words? First we stand and second we make the Sign of the Cross on our foreheads, our lips, and our hearts, in imitation of the priest repeating with him as we do, "May the word of God be in our minds, on our lips, and in our hearts." Because a different part of the life of Christ is read every day, the Gospel changes each day. God the Son speaks to us and instructs us in the Gospel.

God speaks to us through scripture—it is His living Word which He desires to share with us here today. As a preacher, the priest's role is to open the scriptures up to his people. He does so in the Sermon.

The *Credo* is usually the final prayer of preparation for the Great Sacrifice. In this prayer, the *Nicene Creed,* we profess our faith in the teachings of Christ and His

Church. In another Creed which you know better, The Apostles' Creed, we do this, too. Why is it called the Apostles' Creed? Refer to your first unit if you cannot recall this answer. Now, why do you think this act of faith is called the Nicene Creed? It received the name from Nicaea, the place where the Council was held at which this prayer was composed. Perhaps you would like to find the Nicene Creed in a missal and compare it with the Apostles' Creed. If you do, tell the class how they are alike and how they are different.

In the early Church, after the *Credo*, the catechumens, that is those who were not yet baptized, were not permitted to be present for the most solemn part of the Mass. At this point they had to leave the church.

FOR ME TO STUDY

1. Explain what the Epistle is.
2. Who wrote the Epistles?
3. For a Sunday Mass, where do the first and second readings come from?
4. Who wrote the Gospels?
5. How do you show your reverence for the Gospel?
6. Who instructs us in the Gospel?
7. What is the *Credo*?
8. Who were the catechumens?
9. Be prepared to use these terms in a sentence:

   Epistle
   Gospel
   Catechumens
   Nicene Creed

FOR ME TO REMEMBER

1. The first reading is taken from the old Testament
2. The second reading is taken from the New Testament, usually from an Epistle.
3. The Gospel is taken from the account of the life and teachings of Christ written by the four Evangelists.
4. In the first and second readings, and in the Gospel, God speaks to us.
5. God also speaks to us through the priest in the sermon.
6. The Credo is an act of faith. It is the Nicene Creed.
7. The catechumens, people who were not yet baptized, had to leave the church after the Credo.

FOR ME TO DO

1. God teaches us through our priests. Let us say a prayer often that God will bless the priests of our parish and their work.
2. Find the Nicene Creed in my missal; read it slowly, devoutly, and thoughtfully.
3. Pray for an open mind and heart to receive the lessons in the priest's sermon.

LESSON 39

We Offer

When the preparatory prayers are completed, the priest removes the veil which up to this time has kept the *chalice* covered. He is about to begin the *first* principal part of the sacrifice, the Offertory. At the Last Supper, Christ offered bread and wine and now the priest does the same.

The altar servers leave their places and walk to a table on which rest two cruets, one containing wine, the other water. Each takes a cruet and stands at the side while the priest raises the paten bearing the large host and offers it to God. He takes the cruet containing wine and pours some of it into his chalice.

He blesses the water and pours a few drops into the chalice with the wine. What happens when the water is added to the wine? Would you be able to separate it from the wine? No, the two are united and are as one. Let us listen to the priest as he offers the chalice to almighty God. "We offer to Thee, O Lord . . ." The priest is making the offering but he says, "We offer," not "I offer." He is telling us that each of us who is present at the Mass is united with him in offering the sacrifice. Indeed the whole Church joins with him. The Offertory makes the oneness of the Church visible. In the prayers recited

Why is water added to the wine?

The wine represents Christ's divinity and the drops of water represent His humanity. Just as Christ partakes in our humanity, so we, by offering ourselves to God and receiving His life within us, partake in His divinity. Both wine and water are blessed as a testament to the union of Christ's divine and human nature.

TERMS TO KNOW

- Chalice
- Cruet
- Paten
- Offertory
- Lavabo

during the Offertory, we hear the priest make the offering in his name, in the name of all those present, and also of all Christians. The entire Mystical Body of Christ, that is, every Christian in every part of the world, is united to the priest and all the faithful in the Holy Sacrifice of the Mass each time it is offered.

When the priest has offered the bread and wine, he prays and washes his fingers. This is called the *Lavabo*. Then the priest prays again, this time asking the Blessed Trinity to accept the offering in remembrance of the Passion, Resurrection, and Ascension of Jesus Christ.

FOR ME TO STUDY

1. What does the mixture of water and wine symbolize?
2. How does the Offertory show the oneness of the Church?
3. What is the Lavabo?
4. Can you use these words correctly?
   Offertory
   Lavabo
   Partake

FOR ME TO REMEMBER

1. The Offertory is the first principal part of the Mass.
2. The wine represents Christ's divinity, the water represents His humanity.
3. The mixture of wine and water symbolizes the union of Christ's divine and human natures.
4. The priest makes the offering in his name, in the name of all those present, and also for all Christians.

5. The entire Mystical Body of Christ is united in the Holy Sacrifice of the Mass each time it is offered.
6. Each ceremony has a special significance especially for me.

FOR ME TO DO

1. The Holy Sacrifice of the Mass is being offered now someplace in the world. Let us stop and unite ourselves with the Mass being offered at this minute.
2. Make a contribution at Mass to remind myself that it is my duty to give things to God as well as ask Him for favors.

LESSON 40

We Sacrifice

The bread and wine have been offered to God and soon they will be changed into the body and blood of our Lord. Christ Himself will be present on the altar offering Himself as our Victim to God. How this thought moves us to give praise and glory to God! What gratitude fills our hearts.

We express these feelings of love, praise, and gratitude to God in the ***Preface*** of the Mass. The Preface ends with the *Sanctus*, a prayer of continued praise and glory. Find the *Sanctus* in your missal. When were the concluding words of this prayer first sung?

We are approaching the most solemn act of the Mass, the *Consecration*, the *second* principal part of the Mass.

When the bee has gathered the dew of heaven and the earth's sweetest nectar from the flowers, it turns it into honey, then hastens to its hive. In the same way, the priest, having taken from the altar the Son of God (who is as the dew from heaven, and true son of Mary, flower of our humanity), gives him to you as delicious food.

ST. FRANCIS DE SALES

At this time the Church interrupts the sacrifice to remind us that in the Mass we are all united and share in its infinite merits. We pray for all the clergy of the *Church Militant*. You should remember especially, the pope, your bishop, and all the priests of your own parish.

We pray next for all our friends, relatives, and other members of the Church Militant. Pray here especially for your parents and members of your family, your teachers, and all who help you to know and love God.

We remember next the *Church Triumphant*. Whom does this include?

The priest extends his hands over the chalice and again asks God to accept his offering. The bell is sounded. The priest continues his prayer and makes the Sign of the Cross over the bread and wine. We watch the priest as he bows low and begins the sacred act of Consecration.

The priest is about to fulfill the command Christ gave on the first Holy Thursday night. Do you remember what that was? The priest recalls what Christ did and now he himself is about to perform the same act. He says: "*This is My body*." He genuflects, elevates the Sacred Host for us to see and adore, then genuflects again. The altar server rings the bell again. You should look up at the Host and say: "*My Lord and my God*."

Immediately after this the priest consecrates the wine. You see him again bow low and pray: "*This is the chalice of My blood*." The priest genuflects, raises the chalice, and genuflects. Once again the altar server rings the bell. We again look up at the chalice and say: "*My Lord and my God*." Everything is still, solemn, and very quiet. We have just witnessed a great marvel! Christ becomes present on our altar, where He offers Himself to God as our victim of sacrifice.

In the prayers which follow we ask God to accept our offering. We recall the Old Testament sacrifices and ask that, as God accepted them, He will now accept our sacrifice.

We then recite three more prayers of remembrance, the first in memory of the *Church Suffering*. The second is said in remembrance of the Church Militant, especially of us sinners. The third is said to remind us that it is through Christ that we receive all good things.

The minor elevation follows, in which we see the priest raise the Host and Chalice once more. What does the word "minor" tell you about this elevation of the Host and Chalice? When did you see the major elevation?

FOR ME TO STUDY

1. Explain what the Preface is.
2. What is the Sanctus?
3. What are the three remembrance prayers which are said before the Consecration?
4. Explain the actions and prayers of the priest at the Consecration.
5. What should your actions and prayers be at the Consecration?
6. What Old Testament sacrifices are recalled?
7. What three remembrance prayers follow the Consecration?
8. What is the minor elevation?
9. Explain these terms as they are used in this lesson.

Preface	*Church Suffering*
Consecration	*Sanctus*
Church Militant	*Church Triumphant*
Minor Elevation	

FOR ME TO REMEMBER

1. In the Preface we give thanks and praise and glory to God.
2. The Sanctus is the conclusion of the Preface.
3. The Consecration is the most solemn act of the Mass.

FOR ME TO DO

1. Think about the great marvel that comes to pass in the Consecration of the Mass. Thank God in my own words for sending His Son to offer Himself for us.
2. Be as attentive as possible at this part of the Mass.
3. Praise the Holy Presence of God at the moment of the elevation by reciting such prayers as, "My Lord and my God."

LESSON 41

We Receive

At the Offertory, the bread and wine are offered to God. In the Consecration, the bread and wine are changed into the body and blood of Christ. We now approach the Communion, in which we receive Jesus Christ into our hearts. This is the *third* principal part of the Mass.

The Communion of the Mass begins with a prayer which was taught to the Apostles by Christ Himself. We recite it very often. It is the *Our Father*.

The priest continues the last petition of the *Our Father* into the next prayer asking God to deliver us ". . . from all evils, past, present and to come . . ." He then breaks the Host into three

Seven Petitions of the Our Father

You may never have thought of it like this, but the Our Father is a series of petitions, or requests. There are seven of these petitions. We ask that:

(1) God's name be "hallowed"
(2) His Kingdom comes
(3) His will be done
(4) He gives us our daily bread
(5) He forgives us our trespasses
(6) He leads us not into temptation
(7) He delivers us from evil

parts, makes the Sign of the Cross over the chalice with the small *particle*, and prays that the peace of God may be always with us. The priest then drops the *particle*, or smaller piece, of the Host into the chalice.

In the next part of the Mass we are reminded of a saint whom we should remember because he announced Christ as the Lamb of God. Do you recall who the saint was? We hear the priest repeat the title he gave to Christ saying: "Lamb of God, who takest away the sins of the world, have mercy upon us; . . . grant us peace." We join the priest in a plea for mercy and peace.

The priest now makes his own personal preparation for Holy Communion. He takes the Host into his hands, asks God to forgive him his sins, and prays that he may not receive the body and blood of Christ unworthily.

Do you recall the story of the centurion who asked Christ to heal his servant? We, along with the priest, repeat the centurion's words just before he receives Christ in Holy Communion, saying: "Lord, I am not worthy that you should enter under my roof: but only say the word, and my soul shall be healed" (Lk. 7:6–7).

He receives the Sacred Host and recites a prayer of thanksgiving. He then takes the chalice and receives the precious blood of Christ. Now those present at the Mass can go to Holy Communion and share in the Sacrificial Banquet of the Holy Eucharist. Let us recall that *Holy Communion is the receiving of Jesus Christ in the sacrament of the Holy Eucharist.*

You have received Holy Communion many times. How do you prepare your soul for this great gift? When a guest comes to your home, how do you prepare? Perhaps you tidy up your room, put out fresh flowers, prepare a meal to share. What can you do to prepare for the coming of Christ into your soul? Do you spend time in silence meditating on the life of Christ? Do you repent for the wrongs you have committed? Do you praise God for His wonderful works? You know that *to receive Holy Communion worthily it is necessary to be free from mortal sin, to have a right intention, and to obey the Church's laws on fasting before Holy Communion. But if a Catholic is in danger of death or is trying to protect the Blessed Sacrament from insult, no fast is required before receiving the Holy Eucharist.*

This fast which we keep before going to Holy Communion is called the Eucharistic Fast. Drinking water does not break this fast. Anyone may drink water before going to Holy Communion. *Before Holy Communion we must fast by not taking any food or liquids for one hour, except water, which may be taken at any time.*

You recall, too, that *he who knowingly receives Holy Communion in mortal sin receives the body and blood of Christ; but he does not receive His graces, and he commits a grave sin of sacrilege.* You remember that a sacrilege is an offense against a sacred object, or person—here, our Lord Himself.

We should prepare ourselves for Holy Communion by thinking of our Divine Redeemer, whom we are about to receive, and by making fervent acts of faith, hope, love, and contrition.

The priest then carries Christ to all who are waiting to receive Him in Holy Communion. When Christ comes into our hearts how

truly can we say: "It is now no longer I that live, but Christ lives in me" (Gal. 2:20). One who realizes this will quickly see that *it is well to receive Holy Communion often, even daily, because this close union with Jesus Christ is the greatest aid to a holy life.*

After receiving any gift, our sense of gratitude urges us to give thanks. How much more when we have received the most treasured of all gifts, namely, Jesus Christ Himself! The Mass provides prayers of thanksgiving but we should also spend some time saying thanks in our own words. *After Holy Communion we should spend some time adoring our Lord, thanking Him, renewing our promises of love and of obedience to Him, and asking Him for blessings for ourselves and others.*

The priest returns to the middle of the altar, kisses it, and turns toward the people to salute them once more with the touching words: "The Lord be with you." We then hear him say: *"Ite, Missa est,"* which means: "Go, this is the dismissal," or more commonly heard, "Go forth the Mass has ended." To which we respond "Deo gratias," that is, "Thanks be to God."

The priest turns once more toward the people and raises his right hand to give the *Last Blessing*, saying as he makes the sign of the cross: "May Almighty God bless you: the Father, the Son, and the Holy Spirit."

If we have received our Lord in Holy Communion, we ought to stay for a short time after Mass to finish our thanksgiving. This will show Christ that we appreciate His great gift to us. As we leave the Church we take with us the graces received and the lessons taught us in the Mass. Throughout the day our actions should show that we are trying to live like Christ in Christ, that is as true members of Christ's Mystical Body.

FOR ME TO STUDY

Catechism Lesson

253. Q. What is Holy Communion?

A. Holy Communion is the receiving of the body and blood of Christ.

254. Q. What is necessary to make a good Communion?

A. To make a good Communion it is necessary to be in the state of grace and to be fasting for one hour from food and all drinks, except water.

255. Q. Does he who receives Communion in mortal sin receive the body and blood of Christ?

A. He who receives Communion in mortal sin receives the body and blood of Christ, but does not receive His grace, and he commits a great sacrilege.

905. Q. **What is the fast necessary for Holy Communion?**

A. The fast necessary for Holy Communion is to abstain from all food, beverages and alcoholic drinks for one hour before Holy Communion. Water may be taken at any time. The sick may take food, non-alcoholic drinks, and any medication up to Communion time.

910. Q. **How shall we know how often we should receive Holy Communion?**

A. We shall know how often we should receive Holy Communion only from the advice of our confessor, by whom we must be guided, and whom we must strictly obey in this.

913. Q. **What should we do after Holy Communion?**

A. After Holy Communion we should spend some time in adoring our Lord, in thanking Him for the grace we have received, and in asking Him for the blessings we need.

FOR ME TO REMEMBER

1. The Communion is the third principal part of the Mass.
2. Holy Communion is the receiving of Jesus Christ in the sacrament of Holy Eucharist.
3. The Eucharistic Fast is the fast we keep in preparation for Holy Communion.
4. Our souls must be free from mortal sin and we must be fasting in order to receive Holy Communion worthily.
5. We should receive Holy Communion as often as possible.
6. We should spend some time after Communion thanking our Lord for coming into our hearts.

7. We should remain in our places until the priest has left the altar.
8. We should carry the graces and lessons of the Mass into all our actions throughout the day.

FOR ME TO DO

1. I cannot receive Jesus Christ in Holy Communion at this moment but I can receive Him in a spiritual Communion. I will tell Jesus how much I love Him and that I want Him to come into my heart. I will say this in my own words.
2. Make the resolution to be in my place for Mass before the priest comes into the sanctuary and to remain there until he has left.
3. On the way home from Church thank God whom I have received in Holy Communion.

Holy Mass: The Perfect Sacrifice

Write your answers on a separate sheet of paper

PART I *Yes or No*

Answer the following questions with Yes or No:

1. Does the altar stone contain relics of martyrs?
2. Is the Credo an act of love?
3. Is Christ the priest and victim in every Mass?
4. Does Christ die again in the Mass?
5. Is the sacrifice of the Mass a perfect sacrifice?
6. Were the sacrifices of the Old Testament perfect sacrifices?
7. Do the prayers of the Ordinary of the Mass change from day to day?
8. Do the Epistles contain the life of Christ?
9. Is the Kyrie a plea for mercy?
10. In the Collect do we tell God we are sorry for our sins?

PART II *Multiple Choice*

Choose the correct answer:

1. The Preface is an introduction to the:
   A. Offertory.
   B. Consecration.
   C. Sanctus.

2. The Sanctus is a prayer of:
   A. petition.
   B. praise.
   C. sorrow.

3. When the priest washes his fingers during Mass, he says the:
   A. Secret.
   B. Lavabo.
   C. Sanctus.

4. The sacrifices of the Old Testament are recalled:
   A. during the Offertory.
   B. just before the Consecration.
   C. just after the Consecration.

5. In the Kyrie, we honor the:
   A. martyrs.
   B. Blessed Trinity.
   C. apostles.

6. The Gloria is a prayer of:
   A. praise.
   B. petition.
   C. sorrow.

7. We partake of the Sacrificial Banquet at the:
   A. Offertory.
   B. Communion.
   C. Consecration.

8. The Confiteor is a prayer of:
   A. faith.
   B. praise.
   C. contrition.

9. Christ's sacrifice on the cross was perfect because:
   A. God loved Christ.
   B. the priest and Victim were perfect.
   C. Christ wanted to make the sacrifice.

10. In the Mass today, we offer ourselves to:
    A. God.
    B. all the saints.
    C. the Blessed Virgin.

PART III *Ordinary or Proper*

On your paper mark with an O the parts of the Mass which belong to the Ordinary, and a P those which belong to the Proper:

1. Confiteor
2. The Readings
3. Gloria
4. Kyrie
5. Introit
6. Lavabo
7. Collect
8. Credo

PART IV *Completion*

Complete the following sentences by supplying the missing words.

1. The Mass is the (1) of the New Law in which (2), through the priest, offers Himself to God in an unbloody manner under the appearances of (3) and (4).
2. The sacrifices of the Old Testament were not completely pleasing to God because the (5) and (6) were not perfect.
3. The bread and wine are changed into Christ's body and blood at the (7).
4. The offering of bread and wine represents the offering of (8) along with the offering of (9).
5. The highest form of worship is the (10).

CHAPTER 21
Penance and Reconciliation: Love and Mercy

LESSON 42

The Sacrament of Penance and Reconciliation

Above the confessional in a certain church there is a large painting of a story you well know. An elderly, richly clothed man is standing with his arms open wide. You can see that he has left the porch of his home to go down to welcome his visitor. Kneeling at his feet is a young, poorly dressed lad. His head is bowed low as if he were asking pardon for something he had done.

You recognize this as the picture of the prodigal son. You remember that in this story, the father saw his son a long way off and ran forward to meet him and to welcome him back home. St. Luke tells us, too, that the father was happy because he had thought his son dead, and now he had, as it were, come back to life.

We know that Christ told the people this parable because He does not want anyone to doubt the infinite mercy of God. He wants us to remember this story when we have sinned. God has not changed. He cannot change. His mercy still awaits us when our souls are dead in sin, or lost to His Church. When we have sinned, especially grievously, and are sorry, we can always go to confession. We can turn back to God to tell Him we are sorry and to ask His pardon.

You know that the sacrament you receive when you go to confession is called Penance and Reconciliation, and that *it's the*

sacrament by which sins committed after Baptism are forgiven.

How We Receive the Sacrament of Penance and Reconciliation

This sacrament is not entirely new to us. We studied it in preparation for our first Holy Communion. Since then we have received the sacrament of Penance and Reconciliation many times. Let us review here the five things that every Catholic must do to receive worthily this great sacrament of God's mercy. *To receive the sacrament of Penance and Reconciliation worthily,* we must first, examine our conscience; second, must have sorrow for our sins; third, must make a firm resolution never more to offend God; fourth, must confess our sins to the priest; and fifth, must accept the penance which the priest gives us.

Examination of Conscience

An examination of conscience is a sincere effort to call to mind all the sins we have committed since our last confession. We have seen that the priest has the power to forgive sins. However, before the priest can

The Institution of the Sacrament of Penance and Reconciliation

Let us recall from Holy Scripture the story of how Christ instituted the sacrament of Penance and Reconciliation. We must go back to the evening of the first Easter Sunday. The Apostles were gathered in Jerusalem. The doors were closed because of fear of the Jews. Jesus came to them: He breathed upon them and said: "Receive the Holy Spirit; whose sins you shall forgive, they are forgiven them; and whose sins you shall retain, they are retained" (Jn. 20:19–23). When Christ spoke those words, He instituted the sacrament of Penance and Reconciliation and gave the Apostles the power to forgive sins. This same power is given to each priest by the bishop during the ceremony of ordination. These same words of Christ are repeated by the bishop to the newly ordained priest. Every priest receives the power to forgive sins.

exercise this power, we must confess our guilt. He acts as a judge, and a judge must know the crime. He must know whether he can forgive, and from what. Therefore, we must make an examination of our conscience and to do this well *we should ask God's help to know our sins and to confess them with sincere sorrow. We can make a good examination of conscience by calling to mind the commandments of God and the precepts of the Church, and by asking ourselves how we may have sinned with regard to them.*

Ask God for the grace to remember the times we have failed to love Him. How have we failed to love our neighbor? If we go to confession every week or every two weeks, it will be quite easy to recall the sins committed since our last confession.

FOR ME TO STUDY

Catechism Lesson

721. Q. What is the sacrament of Penance and Reconciliation?

A. Penance and Reconciliation is a sacrament in which the sins committed after Baptism are forgiven.

741. Q. What must we do to receive the sacrament of Penance and Reconciliation worthily?

A. To receive the sacrament of Penance and Reconciliation worthily we must do five things:

1. We must examine our conscience.
2. We must have sorrow for our sins.
3. We must make a firm resolution never more to offend God.
4. We must confess our sins to the priest.
5. We must accept the penance which the priest gives us.

749. Q. What is the examination of conscience?

A. The examination of conscience is an earnest effort to recall to mind all the sins we have committed since our last worthy confession.

751. Q. How can we make a good examination of conscience?

A. We can make a good examination of conscience by calling to memory the commandments of God, the precepts of the Church, the seven capital sins, and the particular duties of our state in life, to find out the sins we have committed.

- *Why did Christ tell the story of the prodigal son?*

752. Q. What should we do before beginning the examination of conscience?

A. Before beginning the examination of conscience we should pray to God to give us light to know our sins and grace to detest them.

- *Why should we ask for God's help before examining our conscience?*

FOR ME TO REMEMBER

1. The sacrament of Penance and Reconciliation is the sacrament by which sins committed after Baptism are forgiven.
2. The sacrament of Penance and Reconciliation was instituted on the first Easter Sunday.
3. We should ask God's help to know our sins and to be truly sorry for them.
4. We can make a good examination of conscience by recalling the commandments of God and the precepts of the Church and asking ourselves how we may have sinned against them.
5. God is always willing to forgive us our sins, if we are truly sorry for them.

FOR ME TO DO

1. I will examine my conscience as part of my night prayer.
2. I will try to think of God's mercy each time that I get ready to receive the sacrament of Penance and Reconciliation.
3. I will try to check my progress and note my failures.

LESSON 43

Contrition

Therese was crying bitterly. When Mother asked her the cause of her tears, Therese explained that her father had forbidden her to skate out into the street. Because she had disobeyed him, her father was angry and told Therese she could not use the skates for a week. "But, mother," continued Therese, "I'm not crying because I cannot use my skates. I'm sorry that I disobeyed father and caused him to become angry." Would you say that Therese was truly sorry for her disobedience?

You remember, in our last lesson we learned that we must pray for God's help to be sorry for our sins. Another name for true sorrow for sins is contrition. *Contrition is sincere sorrow for having offended God, and hatred for the sins we have committed, with a firm purpose of sinning no more.* From this we learn that contrition means more than mere sorrow for sin. When we realize that it means also a hatred for sin and a firm resolution to sin no more, we understand how very important contrition is. We should never think of confession as a "mere telling" of past sins.

When we think of God's love for us, we realize how important it is for us to hate and to be sorry for all sin, but especially for mortal sin. Is there anything more terrible than mortal sin? You can mention many great evils, yet mortal sin is the greatest. Think of what even one mortal sin does. It gravely offends our Creator, our Redeemer, our God. It keeps us from enjoying God in heaven and condemns us to suffer in hell forever. It brings a loss of all the merits we have ever gained. Therefore, *we should have contrition for mortal sin because it is the greatest of all evils, gravely offends God,* and when we fail to repent, it keeps us separated from God forever. This is the state of a soul in hell: eternal separation from God.

If your friend told you he was sorry he knocked your hat on the floor, would you think he was sincere if he came right back and did the same thing over again? Certainly not! Neither is our contrition sincere unless we firmly resolve not to commit again the sin we have confessed. Our contrition is sincere only if we have a firm purpose of sinning no more.

Venial sin is a lesser offense against God. This does not mean that our sorrow for it should be any less sincere. *We should have contrition for venial sin because it is displeasing to God,* and damages our relationship with Him. Even venial sins greatly disfigure our souls, they blind us to the Truth who is Christ and prevent us from experiencing the joy of a good and holy life on earth and in heaven. If we die with a venial sin on our soul, we must be purified in the fires of purgatory before being able to see God face to face in heaven.

The Consequences of Venial Sin

It can be tempting to think that venial sins are not a big deal. While they are less serious than mortal sins, we should not take venial sins lightly. Venial sins that go unconfessed and which we have little or no contrition for can wound and weaken our soul, making us more vulnerable to temptation and to committing mortal sin. Think of it in terms of someone's physical health. A certain sickness or injury is not as serious as death, but if someone faces enough sickness or injury, their body can still be weakened and their life threatened. The best way to avoid mortal sin is to first avoid venial sin, or confess our venial sins as soon and as often as we can.

Contrition (Sorrow for Sin)

Perfect	Imperfect
Based on love of God	Based on fear of God's punishment
Better than imperfect contrition	Sufficient in confession

Kinds of Contrition

There are two kinds of contrition: perfect contrition and imperfect contrition. Our contrition is perfect when we are sorry for our sins because sin offends God, whom we love above all things for His own sake. Perfect contrition is sorrow for sins based on love of God. We love God for Himself, who is goodness itself and wishes to share His goodness with us if we but let Him. St. Peter had perfect contrition for his sin of denying Christ. St. Mary Magdalen, too, had perfect contrition for her many sins. She was sorry because she realized how her sins offended God who was worthy of all her love. Let us examine our sorrow for sins and see if it is perfect. Are we sorry because our sins offend God whom we love above all things for His own sake?

Our contrition is imperfect when we are sorry for our sins because they are hateful in themselves or because we fear God's punishment. Let us use as an example a child who sins by stealing. Suppose he hates his sin because he feels that it was an evil, hateful thing that he did. He might also be sorry for his sin because he knows that it will be punished by God. If he is sorry for these reasons, his sorrow or contrition is imperfect.

From this we learn that our contrition is perfect or imperfect depending on the reason for our sorrow. It is perfect when we are sorry because we have offended God who is so good and worthy of love. It is imperfect when we are sorry for the more selfish reasons of being afraid of God's punishment or because the sins are hateful in themselves. Sometimes, boys and girls have the idea that contrition is perfect if they recite the Act of Contrition without any mistakes. This does not make our contrition perfect or imperfect. It is the reason why we are sorry that makes the difference. We must mean what we are saying when we recite the Act of Contrition. We should be sorry we have offended God.

Perfect contrition is, of course, always better; but, as you already realize, *to receive the sacrament of Penance and Reconciliation worthily, imperfect contrition is sufficient.* Our sins will be forgiven in confession even though our sorrow is caused by our hatred for the sin or because we fear God's punishment.

If we commit a mortal sin, we should make an act of perfect contrition at once and go to confession as soon as we can. Recall what a mortal sin does to our soul. If we make an act of perfect contrition immediately and resolve to go to confession the first chance we get, we can be quickly restored to God's grace.

Suppose William committed a mortal sin. If he made an act of perfect contrition and resolved to go to confession at once, he would be saved from hell if he died before he could get to confession. This great privilege is like a fire ladder on a burning building. It is a plank after a shipwreck. It will save us in an emergency.

However, *we may not receive Holy Communion after committing a mortal sin, if we merely make an act of perfect contrition; one who has sinned grievously must go to confession before receiving Holy Communion.* Think again about William. The act of perfect contrition would save him in case he should die before getting to confession. But he could not receive Holy Communion until he confessed that mortal sin. This lesson should help us to appreciate more the Act of Contrition which we have learned. Let us say this prayer very slowly. Let us try to find the words that make it an act of perfect contrition.

FOR ME TO STUDY

Catechism Lesson

753. Q. What is contrition, or sorrow for sin?

A. Contrition, or sorrow for sin, is a hatred of sin and a true grief of the soul for having offended God, with a firm purpose of sinning no more.

- *What does contrition include besides sorrow for sin?*

762. Q. Why should we be sorry for our sins?

A. We should be sorry for our sins because sin is the greatest of evils and an offense against God our Creator, Preserver, and Redeemer, and because it shuts us out of heaven and condemns us to the eternal pains of hell.

- *Explain the phrase, "gracely offends God."*

764. Q. How many kinds of contrition are there?

A. There are two kinds of contrition: perfect contrition and imperfect contrition.

765. Q. What is perfect contrition?

A. Perfect contrition is that which fills us with sorrow and hatred for sin, because it offends God, who is infinitely good in Himself and worthy of all love.

767. Q. What is imperfect contrition?

A. Imperfect contrition is that by which we hate what offends God because by it we lose heaven and deserve hell; or because sin is so hateful in itself.

769. Q. Is imperfect contrition sufficient for a worthy confession?

A. Imperfect contrition is sufficient for a worthy confession, but we should endeavor to have perfect contrition.

780. **Q. What sins are we bound to confess?**
A. We are bound to confess all our mortal sins, but it is well also to confess our venial sins.

766. **Q. When will perfect contrition obtain pardon for mortal sin without the sacrament of Penance and Reconciliation?**
A. Perfect contrition will obtain pardon for mortal sin without the sacrament of Penance and Reconciliation when we cannot go to confession, but with the perfect contrition we must have the intention of going to confession as soon as possible, if we again have the opportunity.

- *Can you write the Act of Contrition?*

FOR ME TO REMEMBER

1. We must have contrition for our sins if we want to receive God's forgiveness.
2. Perfect contrition is sorrow for sins because we have offended God whom we love above all things.
3. Imperfect contrition is sorrow for sin because we hate the sin or because we fear God's punishment.
4. Our sins can be forgiven in confession if we have imperfect contrition, but we should always strive for perfect contrition.
5. If we commit a mortal sin we should make an act of perfect contrition immediately.
6. We may not receive Holy Communion after committing a mortal sin until we have confessed that mortal sin.

FOR ME TO DO

1. Recite devoutly the Act of Contrition as part of my night prayers.
2. Ask God to grant me the grace of perfect sorrow for sin.
3. Devote at least five minutes before confession to reflect on my shortcomings and pray for the grace of contrition.
4. Pray to St. Peter or St. Mary Magdalen to help me have sorrow for my sins.

LESSON 44

Confession

Boys and girls do not usually say that they are going to receive the sacrament of Penance and Reconciliation, but rather, that they are going to confession. Actually, confession is only one part of the sacrament, one of five parts, as we know. *Confession is telling our sins to a priest in order to receive God's forgiveness.*

What sins are we bound to confess? If we have committed venial sins only, it is not required that we confess them. We have not lost sanctifying grace. When we recall, however, that venial sins offend God and prevent us from experiencing the joy of a holy life, we should be glad to confess them, to tell God we are sorry for them, and to receive forgiveness. In such a confession of devotion, the sacrament of Penance and Reconciliation increases sanctifying grace. The Church encourages us, therefore, to confess our venial sins even though it is not necessary to do so.

If we have committed a mortal sin, we have lost sanctifying grace and it is necessary to tell that sin in confession. The sacrament then restores (gives back) sanctifying grace to us.

It could happen that we would forget a sin during our confession. We should not become anxious. God is merciful and has promised His forgiveness to those who ask for it. If we have forgotten to confess a particularly grave sin, we should bring it up in our next confession. This shows our love for God and our desire to be in full communion with the Church. Being completely honest in our confession is important. It helps us to form the habit of promptly admitting when we're wrong which in turn helps us to grow in the virtue of humility—a necessary foundation for the Christian life. The sacrament of Penance and Reconciliation "reconciles" us with Christ and His Church, and it conforms our minds and hearts to God's holy will. What a wonderful gift! How important it is for us to carefully recall our shortcomings and to have the courage to be completely honest in all we have done or failed to do.

A bad confession has an effect on the soul which might be compared to the effect which the wrong kind of medicine would have on the body. The wrong medicine would cause harm, not good; so, too, a bad confession does harm, not good.

A person who, through fear or shame, knowingly keeps back a mortal sin does himself great harm. To regain the state of grace here is what he must do: first, he must tell the priest he has made a bad confession; second, he must tell the sin he has kept back; third, he must tell the sacraments he has received since the bad confession; fourth, he must confess all mortal sins committed since the last good confession.

Jerome missed Mass on Sunday to go fishing with a friend. When he went to confession on the following Saturday, he was ashamed to tell his mortal sin to the priest. He confessed only his venial sins. The next morning he received Holy Communion. By the following Saturday, Jerome was sorry he had made a bad confession. Can you tell what Jerome would have to do in his next confession?

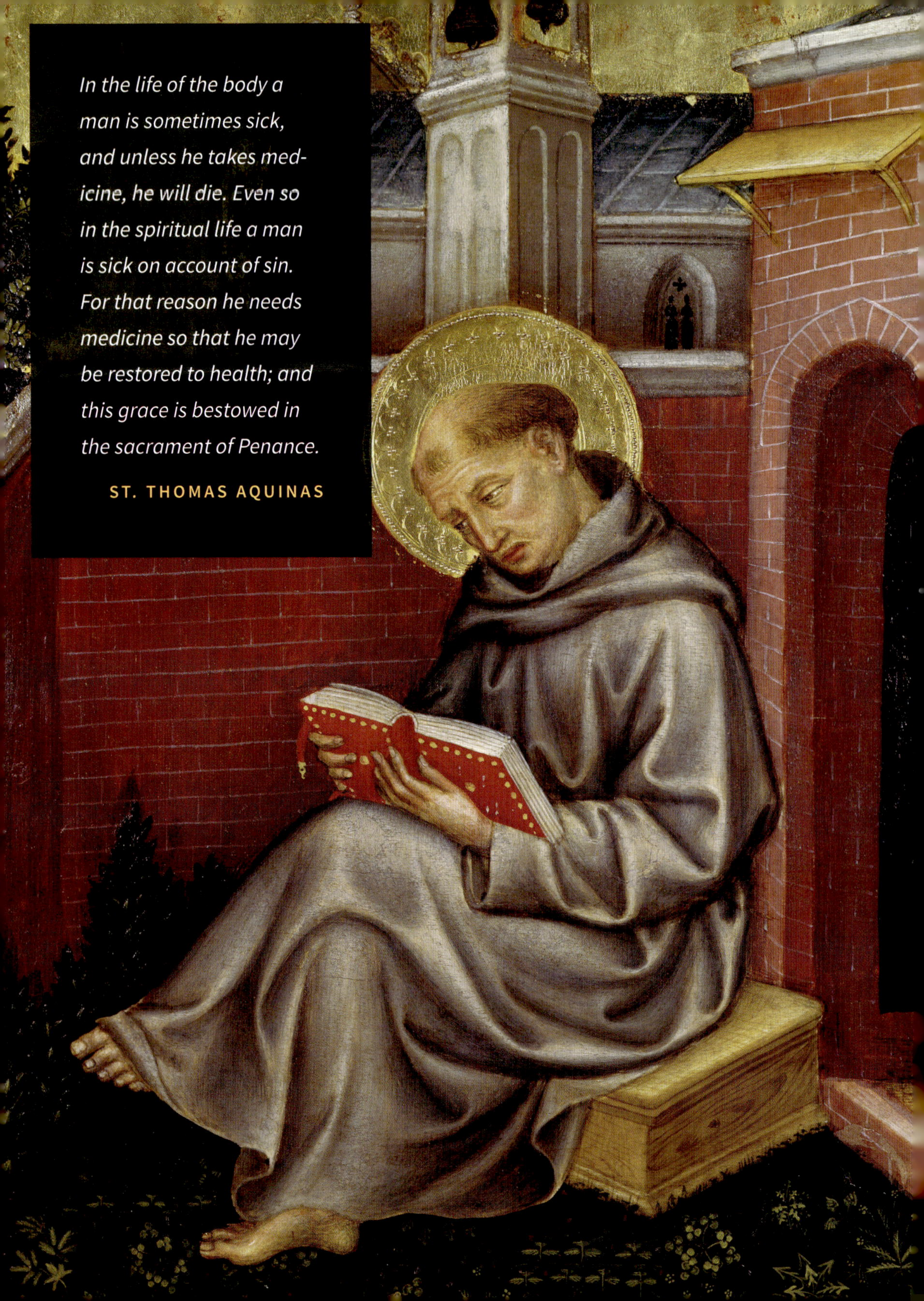

In the life of the body a man is sometimes sick, and unless he takes medicine, he will die. Even so in the spiritual life a man is sick on account of sin. For that reason he needs medicine so that he may be restored to health; and this grace is bestowed in the sacrament of Penance.

ST. THOMAS AQUINAS

FOR ME TO STUDY

Catechism Lesson

776. **Q. What is confession?**

A. Confession is the telling of our sins to a duly authorized priest, for the purpose of obtaining forgiveness.

781. **Q. Why is it well to confess also the venial sins we remember?**

A. It is well to confess also the venial sins we remember 1) because it shows our hatred of all sin, and 2) because it is sometimes difficult to determine just when a sin is venial and when mortal.

794. **Q. May a person who has forgotten to tell a mortal sin in confession go to Holy Communion before going again to confession?**

A. A person who has forgotten to tell a mortal sin in confession may go to Communion before again going to confession, because the forgotten sin was forgiven with those confessed, and the confession was good and worthy.

798. **Q. What must he do who has willfully concealed a mortal sin in confession?**

A. He who has willfully concealed a mortal sin in confession must not only confess it, but must also repeat all the sins he has committed since his last worthy confession.

- *What do we mean by a bad confession?*
- *Explain how a bad confession does harm rather than good.*

FOR ME TO REMEMBER

1. We must confess our sins to a priest to obtain forgiveness.
2. We must confess all mortal sins.
3. It is well to confess our venial sins.
4. We may receive Holy Communion if we have forgotten to confess a mortal sin because the sin is forgiven.
5. If we remember that mortal sin at a later time, we must confess it.
6. We make a bad confession if we knowing keep back a mortal sin.
7. The priest is bound by the seal of the confessional.
8. A person who knowingly has kept back a mortal sin in confession must confess that he has made a bad confession, tell the sin he has kept back, mention the sacraments he has received since that time, and confess all the other mortal sins he has committed since his last good confession.

FOR ME TO DO

1. Look often at the crucifix and recall how much Christ suffered for our sins.
2. Pray daily for the grace to make a good confession.
3. If I am tempted to hold back a serious sin, remember how falsehoods keep me from experiencing the joy of a holy life and how ashamed I will be before the whole world on Judgment Day if I die in mortal sin.
4. Memorize the manner of making a good confession.

LESSON 45

How to Make a Good Confession

After a good confession we know that we are no longer displeasing to God. At home when we have done something wrong, we always feel better after we have told our parents about it and have expressed our sorrow, like Ruth in this story:

While Ruth was dusting the furniture in the living room she broke a vase. This would not have happened if she had been watching what she was doing. Then she went to the store for mother and came back without the thing mother wanted most. A little later, while she was playing in the basement, she carelessly kicked over a can of paint and ruined the lumber Father

"Bless me, Father, for I have sinned"

intended to use. These, plus a few similar mishaps, caused mother and father to be very angry with their thoughtless little girl. Naturally, Ruth felt very bad and by the end of the day she was most unhappy. Before going to bed Ruth told her mother and father that she was sorry for all the trouble she had caused. They were happy to hear her admit her faults, and forgave her readily. Now everything was all right again! Ruth went to bed feeling happy and good.

Our conscience allows us no peace when we have offended God by breaking His laws. But when we tell God we are sorry for our offenses against Him and when the priest makes the sign of the cross over us forgiving our sins, God forgives us and we leave the confessional feeling happy and good.

Examining Our Conscience

In order to make a good confession, *before entering the confessional, we should prepare ourselves by taking time to examine our conscience, to have sorrow for our sins, and to make up our minds not to commit them again.*

While we are young, we should form the habit of always allowing ourselves plenty of time to prepare to receive the sacrament of Penance and Reconciliation properly. Sometimes thoughtless boys and girls rush into church and into the confessional without the proper preparation. This could lead to a bad confession because through carelessness they might miss a serious sin, or might not have the necessary sorrow.

Confessing Our Sins

When we have completed our preparation, we should quietly await our turn to enter the confessional, staying far enough away from the confessional so as not to be able to hear what is being said. During this time we should show our reverence and appreciation by remaining quiet and prayerful. When our turn comes, we should enter and wait until the priest is ready. We know *that should begin our confession in this manner: Entering the confessional, we kneel, and making the sign of the cross we say to the priest: "Bless me, Father, for I have sinned"; and then we tell how long it has been since our last confession.*

We ask the priest to bless us that we may confess our sins properly and receive forgiveness. The priest can tell how often we go to confession from the length of time since our last confession. If we say it is one or two weeks since our last confession, Father will know we go to confession frequently. If we tell him it is two or three months, he may question us and advise us to go more often.

After telling the time of our last confession, if we have committed any mortal sins since that time, we must confess them and also any that we may have forgotten to tell in past confessions, telling the number and nature of each; we may also confess any venial sins we wish to mention.

If we cannot remember the exact number of our mortal sins, we should tell the number as nearly as possible, or say how often we have committed the sins in a day, a week, a month, or a year. The reason for telling the number of times we commit a particular sin is to help the priest judge the condition of our soul, and be able to give us the proper advice and penance. The priest serves as both judge and physician.

Diagnosing Our Own Sickness

Some people explain the sacrament of Penance and Reconciliation by comparing it to a visit to the doctor. We are sick and so we visit a doctor, the priest, who gives us medicine, the healing grace of Christ, to make us better again. But when we go to the doctor, he tells us what is wrong with us after examining us. In confession, *we have to say what is wrong with us.* Only if we are willing to diagnose ourselves, our own sins and weaknesses, is the medicine of God's grace able to heal us.

For instance, if we tell the priest that we have lied many times within a week, he will know that we need help to overcome that sin. In confession the priest takes the place of God and whatever the priest tells us to do to become more perfect is what God Himself wishes us to do.

Additionally, being specific with the sins we have committed helps us to know ourselves, that is to know our weaknesses and our strengths. Knowledge of self is crucial if we hope to avoid near occasions of sin and seek opportunities to grow in virtue and holiness.

We have already learned that we must confess our mortal sins: however, *when we have committed no mortal sin since our last confession, we should confess our venial sins or some sin told in a past confession, for which we are again sorry*. The fact that we say we should confess a sin told in a past confession does not mean that the sin was not forgiven. The sin was forgiven but by confessing it again we tell God again that we are still sorry for that sin. Remember that sorrow for sin is of the greatest importance. The more sorrow we have for our sins the greater is our love of God.

To include sins which may be forgotten *we should end our confession by saying: "For these sins and all the sins of my past life, I am sorry."* Here we see again, how the sacrament of Penance and Reconciliation is truly one of mercy and love. Almighty God forgives even the sins that we, in our weakness, might forget to confess.

After confessing our sins, we should answer truthfully any question the priest asks, and accept the penance he has given us. A doctor cannot help us when we are sick if we refuse to tell him what our trouble is. In confession, when the priest questions us about our sins he is either trying to get some information he needs so that he can give us absolution, or he is trying to help us. If we do not give him the information he needs, it may lead to a bad confession.

The penance which the priest gives is to make up in small part for the sins we have committed; therefore, it is necessary that we accept the penance the priest gives us.

When the priest has heard our sins and given us advice concerning them, he asks us to repeat our act of contrition. While we are again telling God how sorry we are for having offended Him, the priest says the words of absolution and makes the sign of the cross over us on behalf of Christ who forgives us our sins. *When the priest is giving us absolution, we should say from our heart the act of contrition in a tone to be heard by him.* In the confessional we usually find a crucifix. This will help us to say the act of contrition from our heart because it reminds us how greatly Christ suffered to atone for our sins.

We have gone to God and told Him the sins we have committed. We have told Him, too, that we are sorry. In His kindness and mercy He forgives us. We leave the confessional knowing that God has done us a great favor. He has given us many graces. He has given us another chance to live every day more closely united to Him by love.

We must realize that God has given us a very great gift. We say "gift," because God has given us a present that we do not really deserve. God gives it to us because He loves us: the sacrament of Penance and Reconciliation is truly a great gift. *After leaving the confessional we should return thanks to God for the sacrament we have received and do our penance.*

Saying Our Penance

We should say our penance as soon as we leave the confessional; however, if for some good reason we cannot remain in church to say our penance, we should say it as soon as we can. If we do not hear the penance, we should ask the priest to repeat it. If, after we have left the confessional, we forget what prayers the priest has asked us to say, it is well to say the penance the priest usually gives us.

Perhaps you recall the story of the ten lepers whom our Lord cured. As you know our Lord lamented that only one of them returned to thank Him. Each time we go to confession, God cures us, too, of our spiritual illness. Let us be like the one leper who returned to give thanks to God.

I give you thanks for the exceeding goodness which you have now shown me in so graciously pardoning all my sins

The Purpose of Our Penance

You may wonder why you have to complete a penance to complete the effects of this sacrament. You already confessed your sins and received absolution, so why the penance? Some theologians have explained it this way: Imagine your sins are like nails hammered into a wall. When we confess our sins and receive absolution from the priest, it is as if those nails have been pulled out. But the holes left from the nails are still left behind. In a similar way, though our sins are gone, the effects of our sins are still left behind. We have still created habits of sin in our soul which make us more prone to repeat them. The penance, then, is the process of filling in those nail holes, of making our souls whole and healthy again so that we are not prone to repeating the same sins. Remember this the next time you complete your penance!

FOR ME TO STUDY

Catechism Lesson

742. Q. **What should we pray for in preparing for confession?**
A. In preparing for confession we should pray to the Holy Spirit to give us light to know our sins and to understand their guilt; for grace to detest them; for courage to confess them and for strength to keep our resolutions.

825. Q. **What should we do on entering the confessional?**
A. On entering the confessional we should kneel, make the Sign of the Cross, and say to the priest, "Bless me, Father, for I have sinned."

828. Q. **After telling the time of our last confession what should we do?**
A. After telling the time of our last confession we should confess all the mortal sins we have since committed, and all the venial sins we may wish to mention.

832. Q. What must we do when the confessor asks us questions?

A. When the confessor asks us questions we must answer them truthfully and clearly.

833. Q. What should we do after telling our sins?

A. After telling our sins we should listen with attention to the advice which the confessor may think proper to give.

838. Q. What should we do while the priest is giving us absolution?

A. While the priest is giving us absolution we should from our heart renew the Act of Contrition.

- *Why must we say the penance the priest gives us?*
- *Explain how the sacrament of Reconciliation is a true gift.*

FOR ME TO REMEMBER

1. A good confession increases or restores sanctifying grace.
2. In order to make a good confession, we must take time to prepare ourselves properly; that is, to examine our conscience, to have sorrow for our sins, and to resolve firmly not to commit them again.
3. We should tell as nearly as possible the number of times we committed a particular sin.
4. We should include sins we have forgotten by adding that we are sorry for all the sins of our past life.
5. We must answer truthfully any question the priests asks.

6. We must accept the penance the priest gives us in confession.
7. When the priest is giving us absolution, we should say the act of contrition sincerely and with love.
8. After leaving the confessional we should say our penance.
9. The sacrament of Penance and Reconciliation is a great gift from God. We must thank Him sincerely after we have received this gift.

FOR ME TO DO

1. Say a prayer of thanksgiving to God for the sacrament of Penance and Reconciliation.
2. Make the resolution to receive the sacrament of Penance and Reconciliation frequently.
3. Set a definite time to go to confession—every week, every two weeks.

CHAPTER 22

Temporal Punishment and Indulgences

One day, Timmy decided to practice pitching for an upcoming baseball team tryout. Timmy took his glove and his baseball and began his routine exercises. Timmy, however, was not mindful of his surroundings. While aiming for a nearby tree, he accidentally threw the baseball right into the window of his house. Timmy searched for his parents, and upon finding them, immediately apologized for his mistake. Timmy's mother and father forgave him, but still expected Timmy to fix the damage he had caused. The effects of sin are very much like this broken window. Even when we are forgiven, punishment is deserved, and reparation still needs to be made. Timmy used his allowance to pay for the broken window. This meant that Timmy could not spend his money on anything else until the window was fixed.

LESSON 46

Punishment Due to Sin

Timmy's story gives us an example of mistakes which we (of our own accord) can make up for. But when we sin against God, we need His help to make up for the damage. Like the baseball, our sins (even after they're forgiven) cause damage. When we completely reject God, we have sinned mortally, and the damage is eternal. This means it deserves an eternal and a temporal punishment. Venial sin deserves a temporal punishment either on earth or in purgatory. We know that eternal means *lasting forever*, and temporal, *for a time*. When we receive the sacrament of Penance and Reconciliation worthily, our sins are forgiven, eternal punishment is taken away and some if not all of the temporal punishment. At times some of the temporal punishment remains. This can be taken away by our own penances during life; if not, then it must be purified through suffering in purgatory.

What an Indulgence Is

Christ, in His great love for us, has left to His Church a very special means of taking away this temporal punishment for sin. This we call an *indulgence. An indulgence is the taking away of the temporal punishment due to sins already forgiven.*

Everything Christ did while He lived here in this world was deserving of infinite merit, since every act of Christ was infinitely pleasing to God. Since Christ did not need these merits for

Himself, He put them into a great spiritual treasury that they might be used by others. Our Blessed Lady and many of the saints had merits over and above what they needed and these, too, were put into Christ's spiritual bank, the treasury of the Church. Christ gave to His Church, through St. Peter and his successors, the key to this storehouse of merit. We may draw on these merits to pay our debt of temporal punishment. We do this when we receive an indulgence.

Kinds of Indulgences

There are two kinds of indulgences, plenary and partial. Plenary means full or complete. Therefore, *a plenary indulgence is the remission of all the temporal punishment due to our sins.* If we gain a plenary indulgence all the temporal punishment due to our sins is taken away. Why do Catholics hope to obtain a plenary indulgence at the hour of their death?

A partial indulgence is the remission of part of the temporal punishment due to our sins. This means that only part of the punishment due to sin is taken away.

How much punishment is taken away by each indulgence? That is a question which will be answered only when we meet God. Remember, sin is an offense against an infinite God. No one knows just how much punishment a sin will receive. Neither can one tell how much punishment is taken away by an indulgence. How much I receive from an indulgence depends partly on me, too—my fervor, my devotion.

How to Gain Indulgences

You probably already know the answer to the question, "What must I do to *receive* the benefit of these wonderful gifts of the Church's treasury?" *To receive an indulgence for ourselves we must be in the state of grace, desire to receive the indulgence, and perform the works required.* Let us see what each of these requirements means.

We can readily understand the first requirement. "To be in the state of grace" means to be free from mortal sin. We know that unless we are free from mortal sin, we can do nothing deserving of merit.

The second requirement is that we have the desire to receive the indulgence. The Church grants indulgences for many devout acts and prayers which we use in our everyday lives. Sometimes, however, we fail to make the intention of receiving these indulgences. An indulgence is only given when intentionally asked for.

TERMS TO KNOW

- Plenary Indulgence
- Partial Indulgence
- temporal punishment
- remission
- eternal punishment

What do we mean by performing the works required? How do we know what works to perform? Sometimes we are required to visit a church, and go to confession and Holy Communion, and also say certain prayers for the intention of the Holy Father.

The Meaning of Indulgences to Us

We have learned that indulgences do not take away sin but only the temporal punishment due to sin which has been already forgiven. The more indulgences we can gain in this world, the less punishment we will have to suffer in the next. We may also gain indulgences for a soul in purgatory. Remember, the more souls we help to get out of purgatory, the more friends we will have in heaven to pray for us. Although we may gain indulgences for the souls in purgatory and for ourselves, the Church says we cannot gain them for other living persons.

Since God through His Church offers us this wonderful gift of indulgences, we should use them faithfully so that we may more quickly after death enter into the glory which He has prepared for those who love Him.

FOR ME TO STUDY

Catechism Lesson

839. Q. What is an indulgence?

A. An indulgence is the remission in whole or in part of the temporal punishment due to sin.

- *Explain what is meant by the "spiritual treasury."*

843. Q. How many kinds of indulgences are there?

A. There are two kinds of indulgences—plenary and partial.

844. Q. What is a plenary indulgence?

A. A plenary indulgence is the full remission of the temporal punishment due to sin.

845. Q. Is it easy to gain a plenary indulgence?

A. It is not easy to gain a plenary indulgence, as we may understand from its great privilege. To gain a plenary indulgence, we must hate sin, be heartily sorry for even our venial sins, and have no desire for even the slightest sin. Though we may not gain entirely each Plenary Indulgence we seek, we always gain a part of each; that is, a partial indulgence, greater or less in proportion to our good dispositions.

847. Q. What is a partial indulgence?

A. A partial indulgence is the remission of part of the temporal punishment due to sin.

848. Q. How long has the practice of granting indulgences been in use in the Church, and what was its origin?

A. The practice of granting indulgences has been in use in the Church since the time of the Apostles. It had its origin in the earnest prayers of holy persons, and especially of the martyrs begging the Church for their sake to shorten the severe penances of sinners, or to change them into lighter penances. The request was frequently granted and the penance remitted, shortened or changed, and with the penance remitted the temporal punishment corresponding to it was blotted out.

FOR ME TO REMEMBER

1. An indulgence takes away temporal punishment.
2. We may gain an indulgence for ourselves and the poor souls in purgatory.
3. We cannot gain an indulgence for other living persons.
4. The Catholic Church alone has the power to grant indulgences.

FOR ME TO DO

1. Offer indulgenced prayers for the souls in purgatory.
2. Learn the following prayer

    O Mary, conceived without sin,
    pray for us who have recourse to thee.

Penance and Reconciliation; Temporal Punishment and Indulgences

Write your answers on a separate sheet of paper

PART I *Matching*

Match each term in Column I with its meaning in Column II:

Column I	**Column II**
A. Absolution	1. The prayers which the priest tells us to say as part of the punishment due to our sins
B. Imperfect Contrition	2. Punishment which lasts forever
C. Eternal Punishment	3. The words and actions of the priest when he forgives sins
D. Penance	4. A remission of all temporal punishment due to our sins
E. Perfect Contrition	5. Sorrow for sin
F. Plenary Indulgence	6. Sorrow for sin because we have offended God who is deserving of all our love
G. Contrition	7. The act of thinking back over how we have obeyed or disobeyed the Commandments of God and the precepts of the Church
H. Sincere Sorrow	8. A less serious offense against the law of God.
I. Examination of Conscience	9. Sorrow for sin because we fear the punishment of God
J. Venial Sin	10. True or real sorrow

PART II *Yes or No*

Answer the following questions with Yes or No:

1. Is having sorrow for our sins the most important part of the sacrament of Penance and Reconciliation?
2. Must we be in the state of grace to gain an indulgence?
3. Is perfect contrition sorrow for sins because we have offended God whom we love?
4. Was the sacrament of Penance and Reconciliation instituted at the Last Supper?
5. Should the sacrament of Penance and Reconciliation be received only by those who have committed mortal sin?
6. May one who has not been baptized receive the sacrament of Penance and Reconciliation?
7. Should we pray to the Holy Spirit for help to know our sins?
8. Must we say the penance which the priest gives us?
9. Does the plenary indulgence take away all temporal punishment due to our sins?

PART III *Multiple Choice*

Choose the correct answer:

1. Christ instituted Penance and Reconciliation on the feast of:
   A. the Ascension.
   B. Easter.
   C. Pentecost.

2. The crucifix is usually seen in the confessional because:
   A. it reminds us to be sorry for our sins.
   B. it is a sacramental.
   C. it adds beauty to the confessional.

3. The most important part of confession is:
   A. perfect examination of conscience.
   B. a firm resolution to sin no more.
   C. true sorrow for our sins.

4. We should go to confession often because:
   A. we receive grace each time we go to confession.
   B. it pleases our teacher.
   C. the Church tells us to.

5. A partial indulgence is the remission of:
   A. all.
   B. part.
   C. none of the temporal punishment due to our sins.

6. When the priest is giving us absolution we should say the:
   A. Act of Faith.
   B. Act of Love.
   C. Act of Contrition.

7. If we do not hear the penance which the priest gives us, we should:
   A. ask the priest to repeat it.
   B. say some prayers that we know well.
   C. say any prayer that we like.

8. If we cannot remember the exact number of times that we committed some sin, we should:
   A. tell no number at all.
   B. tell about how many times.
   C. make up a number.

9. The remission of all the temporal punishment due to our sins is a:
   A. temporal indulgence.
   B. partial indulgence.
   C. plenary indulgence.

10. Contrition is:
    A. sincere sorrow for sin.
    B. the desire to sin no more.
    C. the resolution to go to confession often.

PART IV *Matching*

Match the beginnings and endings of the following sentences:

A. Beginnings	**B. Endings**
1. We should receive the sacrament of Penance as often as possible	A. because they too offend God and weaken our souls.
2. The sacrament of Penance and Reconciliation is the sacrament	B. we will firmly resolve not to commit those sins again
3. Our contrition is imperfect when we are sorry for our sins	C. because each time we go to confession we receive special grace.
4. After leaving the confessional, we should say our penance and	D. we must keep away from it.
5. If we knowingly keep back a mortal sin, none of our sins are forgiven and	E. because He is all merciful and wants us to go to heaven.
6. If we are truly sorry for our sins	F. by which sins committed after Baptism are forgiven.
7. If we know that a certain person, place, or thing will lead us into sin	G. because we fear the punishments of God.
8. We should have contrition for venial sins	H. we have committed another mortal sin.
9. Jesus instituted the sacrament of Penance and Reconciliation	I. thank God for the grace He has given us.

CHAPTER 23

Strength and Peace

LESSON 47

Extreme Unction: Anointing of the Sick

Christ instituted the sacraments to bring His grace to us. All during our life these sacraments give us the strength to live in a way that is pleasing to Him. Christ knew that we would need special strength and comfort when we are in danger of death and so He provided another sacrament, Extreme Unction, or as it has been called in more recent times, "Anointing of the Sick."

During our Lord's public life He often sent His disciples ahead of Him into a town or village to prepare the way for His coming. St. Mark tells us about this work in these words: "And going forth they preached . . . and they cast out many devils and anointed with oil many sick people and healed them" (Mk. 6:12–13). This shows us that on the word of Christ the Apostles anointed the sick. They were being prepared by our Lord for what they were later to do in administering the sacrament of Anointing of the Sick.

We learned about the sacrament of Anointing of the Sick from St. James in his Epistle. In it he said, "Is anyone among you sick? Let him bring in the presbyters of the Church, and let them pray over him, anointing him with oil in the name of the Lord. And the prayer of faith will save the sick man and the Lord will raise him up and if he be in sin, they shall be forgiven him" (James 5:14, 15, 16). From this text we learn that: *Anointing of*

the Sick is the sacrament which gives health and strength to the soul and sometimes to the body when we are in danger of death.

The term "extreme" explains itself. "Extreme" means last and "Unction" means anointing. If this is the last anointing, there must have been other sacraments in which there is an anointing. Do you know them?

"Is any man sick among you? Let him bring in the priests of the church" (Jas 5:14).

Viaticum: Provision for the Journey

Viaticum is a Latin word meaning "provision (or food) for the journey." Via is a word that means "way" or "path," so this of course refers to one's path to heaven after death. When we receive Viaticum, we take with us on this journey, through the Eucharist, Christ as our companion. The *Catechism of the Catholic Church* says the following: "Like all the sacraments the Anointing of the Sick is a liturgical and communal celebration, whether it takes place in the family home, a hospital or church, for a single sick person or a whole group of sick persons. It is very fitting to celebrate it within the Eucharist, the memorial of the Lord's Passover. If circumstances suggest it, the celebration of the sacrament can be preceded by the sacrament of Penance and Reconciliation and followed by the sacrament of the Eucharist. As the sacrament of Christ's Passover the Eucharist should always be the last sacrament of the earthly journey, the 'viaticum' for 'passing over' to eternal life" (1517).

Anointing of the Sick, a Sacrament of the Living

Anointing of the Sick is a sacrament of the living and should be received in the state of grace. However, if a Catholic person in mortal sin meets with a serious accident or becomes suddenly very ill, he may be anointed even if unconscious. The mortal sin is forgiven if the person had at least imperfect contrition for his sins before he lost consciousness. This sacrament also takes away venial sin and the remains of sin. In addition, this sacrament strengthens the soul to overcome temptation. Moreover, it takes away temporal punishment due to sin, removes the fear of death, and comforts the soul. The sick person gains strength to bear his suffering and to accept the will of God. Anointing of the Sick often brings a wonderful calm and peace to the sick person. At times it may even help his recovery.

Preparation for the Sacrament

How do we prepare a sick person to receive this comforting sacrament? Every Catholic boy and girl should know.

First of all we should call a priest immediately when a person who has reached the age of reason becomes seriously sick. We should not wait until the sick person is actually dying. Anointing of the Sick is usually administered after the sacraments of Penance and Reconciliation and the Holy Eucharist. The three sacraments together are called "the Last Sacraments."

While awaiting the arrival of the priest, we should prepare the sickroom. It is well to have everything in the room and about the patient neat and clean. We should cover a table with a clean, white cloth and place on it the following:

A crucifix (or have one hanging on the wall above the table)
Two blessed candles (lighted)
Holy water
A white napkin or a small towel
A glass of fresh water and spoon

We meet the priest at the door with a lighted candle if he has the Blessed Sacrament, and lead him immediately to the sickroom. If the sick person wishes to go to confession, all will leave the room while the priest hears his confession. The patient then receives Holy Communion, which is called the Holy Viaticum, meaning, "with you on the journey." After that the sacrament of the Anointing of the Sick is administered.

Administration of the Sacrament

The holy oil that the priest uses in anointing the sick person is blessed by the bishop on Holy Thursday with these words: "Send forth, we beseech Thee, O Lord, the Holy Spirit, Thy Paraclete, from the heavens into this rich olive oil which Thou hast deigned to produce from a flourishing tree for the refreshment of soul and of body; so that for everyone who is anointed with this ointment of heavenly medicine, it may be a protection of soul and of body to dispel all pains and infirmities and all spiritual and physical ailments."

The priest anoints the different parts of the body by which sins are committed. These parts are the five senses: the eyes, ears, nose, mouth, hands, and sometimes the feet. The priest makes the Sign of the Cross on each sense with the holy oil, saying: "Through this holy anointing and His benign mercy, may the Lord pardon thee whatever sins thou has committed by sight (or hearing, smell, taste, and speech, touch, and walking). Amen."

This sacrament may be received many times. If the person anointed recovers, he may receive the sacrament again if he is once more in danger of death. A very old person is always in danger of death and may receive Anointing of the Sick repeatedly. To receive this sacrament one must, however, be in danger of death from sickness, accident, or old age.

A priest may administer this sacrament to a person who has just died. It is not known exactly when the soul leaves the body, so the sacrament may be administered for some hours after apparent death, provided death has been sudden.

A Happy Death

We have nothing to fear in receiving this sacrament. Accordingly we should pray that we may have the privilege of receiving it. St. Joseph is the patron of a happy death, because Christ was present when he died. Let us ask him often during our lives for the grace to receive the last sacraments, that we may, like him, die in the love and company of Jesus and Mary.

FOR ME TO STUDY

Catechism Lesson

956. Q. What is the sacrament of the Anointing of the Sick?

A. Anointing of the Sick is the sacrament which, through the anointing and prayer of the priest, gives health and strength to the soul, and sometimes to the body, when we are in danger of death from sickness.

- *Explain the meaning of the prayer that the bishop says over the Oil of the Sick.*

FOR ME TO REMEMBER

1. Anointing of the Sick is administered by a priest to a baptized Catholic who has reached the use of reason and is in danger of death.
2. St. Joseph is the patron of a happy death.
3. Anointing of the Sick is a sacrament of the living, although it may sometimes take away mortal sin.
4. Christ gave us the sacrament of the Anointing of the Sick so that we might have special strength and peace when we are in danger of death.

FOR ME TO DO

1. Say a prayer to St. Joseph for a happy death.
2. Say prayers for the dying every day.
3. Often ask our Lord to grant me the grace of receiving this sacrament when I am dying.
4. Have a crucifix in my bedroom.

CHAPTER 24
Holy Orders: "Other Christs"

LESSON 48

The Priest

The priest is another Christ. St. Francis once said that if he were to meet a priest and an angel at the same time he would greet the priest first. Why? Because the priest takes Christ's place, whereas the angel is only His messenger. The priest is used by Christ at the altar when he says, "This is My body; this is My blood." In fact, in each sacrament that he administers and in each duty that he performs, the priest acts as a representative of Christ. This great privilege was given to him in the sacrament of Holy Orders. *Holy Orders is the sacrament through which men become priests, and other ministers of the Church.*

Holy Orders

Do you know when this sacrament was instituted? At the Last Supper after our Lord had changed bread and wine into His body and blood, He said to His Apostles, "Do this in remembrance of Me" (Lk. 22:19). With these words He ordained the Apostles priests and gave them the power to offer the Holy Sacrifice of the Mass.

Today, when a young man wishes to be a priest he consults the pastor or his confessor. He then enters a place of study and preparation called a seminary, where after many years the man becomes a deacon and then finally a priest. Here the sacrament of Holy Orders is received in steps over a period of several years.

In the ceremony of ordination to the priesthood, the bishop lays his hands on the young man, calls down upon him the Holy Spirit, anoints his hands, and presents the sacred vessels to him. Through ordination he is made a priest and receives the power to offer the Holy Sacrifice of the Mass, to teach, to govern, and to administer the sacraments.

The sacrament of Holy Orders imprints on the soul of a priest an indelible mark, that is, a mark that remains always. "Thou art a priest forever according to the order of Melchisedech" (Gen. 49:10) are the words which the bishop uses in addressing the newly ordained. This sacrament, like the other sacraments of the living, increases sanctifying grace and gives its own special sacramental grace. This grace enables the priest to perform well the duties of his high calling and to follow closely in the footsteps of His divine Master.

The fullness of the priesthood is conferred by the sacrament of Holy Orders in the consecration of a bishop. Besides the powers of the priest, a bishop also has

In persona Christi

We say that the priest acts "in persona Christi", meaning "in the person of Christ." He is another Christ. This is part of the reason we only have male priests, because Jesus was a man, and a woman cannot act in the place of a man.

the power to ordain other priests, to administer Confirmation, and to rule the Church. In the consecration of a bishop, three bishops must ordinarily take part.

Reverence for the Priest

Those of us who have always gone to a Catholic school, and have been acquainted with a priest most of our lives, sometimes fail to appreciate the high calling of the priesthood. We take priests more or less for granted, just as we do our mother and father. As good Catholics let us never forget the dignity of the priest. Let us remember that some priest baptized us and helped make us children of God. A priest heard our first confession, gave us our First Holy Communion. Through the priests of our own parish we often receive the sacraments of Penance and Reconciliation and Holy Communion. We can show our gratitude to them by always speaking of them with reverence, obeying them in all things, and trying to help them whenever we can.

The Call: Priesthood and Consecrated Celibacy

How would you know if God is calling you to be a priest? This is an important question and every boy should think about it seriously. Although there is no sacrament for those who enter consecrated life as Sisters or Brothers, nevertheless, this life is a state of higher perfection than marriage because of the vows taken. Men and women, in choosing a consecrated life of chastity, poverty, and obedience, become witnesses to eternal life. They live out what we hope to enjoy in heaven. Every Catholic child should pray to know his or her vocation. We must ask our Lord, "Give me holy desires that I may follow them, and in doing so be united to your Holy Will." Choosing to follow the vocation God has given us is a joyful reality. Our hearts should desire the vocation completely. However, often this desire does not come until we are ready to answer the call. In the meantime, our prayer should be for the grace to fulfill our Christian duties as a child and a student.

Our Lord has said, "The harvest indeed is abundant but the laborers are few. Pray therefore the Lord of the harvest to send forth laborers into his harvest" (Mt. 9:37–38). Christ has great need today for Sisters and Brothers in His schools, hospitals, orphanages, homes for the aged, and missions.

A vocation to consecrate one's life is like that of a priest in that it includes a call from God. It is a high honor to be able to work with Christ and for Christ in saving souls in this very unique way. It is a high life that demands sacrifices, but it is one that is filled with rich graces and blessings, and brings great satisfaction.

Christ has said, "And everyone who has left house, or brothers, or sisters, or father or mother, or wife or children, or lands, for My name's sake shall receive a hundredfold, and shall possess life everlasting" (Mt. 19:29).

Would it not be wonderful to have a big brother as a priest? Just imagine being at his Mass, hearing him preach, or receive Holy Communion from his hands. It would be better still to be a priest and offer the Holy Sacrifice of the Mass yourself. Pray often that God may make known to you what your vocation is. Pray that all men and women who are called to consecrate their lives to God will have the courage to follow that invitation and persevere in it.

We must especially pray for this last intention. There are many priests who, through temptation, have not persevered in holiness. In their sin they act like Judas when he betrayed Our Lord. We must pray that our priests stay strong and persevere in a life of grace. We must also pray for the strength to live our Christian faith with zeal even when those in authority have failed us.

FOR ME TO STUDY

Catechism Lesson

978. Q. What is the sacrament of Holy Orders?

A. Holy Orders is a sacrament by which bishops, priests, and deacons of the Church are ordained and receive the power and grace to perform their sacred duties.

992. Q. What is necessary to receive Holy Orders worthily?

A. To receive Holy Orders worthily it is necessary to be in the state of grace, to have the necessary knowledge, and a divine call to this sacred office.

- *Why do we respect a priest?*
- *Who were the first priests?*
- *Discuss the chief duties of a priest.*
- *What qualities must a young man have to become a priest? In whom is the fullness of the priesthood?*
- *What other consecrated vocations are there besides that of priests?*

FOR ME TO REMEMBER

1. A priest is "another Christ."
2. The priest receives special graces to perform the duties of his calling.
3. A man at ordination is made a priest forever.
4. Good Catholics always speak of a priest with reverence because he is another Christ.

FOR ME TO DO

1. Say a prayer every day for the grace to know God's will and for the strength to do it.
2. Often say a prayer for the priests.
3. Know that God wants my happiness and reveals His will through the desires of a heart kept pure.

CHAPTER 25
Matrimony: Lawful Marriage

The last named of the seven sacraments is Matrimony. You know that Matrimony is the sacrament by which a baptized man and a baptized woman bind themselves for life in a lawful marriage and receive the grace to carry out their duties.

LESSON 49

Christ Institutes Matrimony

Do you remember the wedding at Cana to which our Lord, His Blessed Mother, and the Apostles were invited, and at which the wine ran out? You remember, I am sure, how at the request of His Mother, Christ changed water into wine. How kind our Lord was to perform this miracle. He did not want the bride and groom to be embarrassed on their wedding day. Our Lord by His presence and His miracle showed great respect for the holy state of matrimony. He wished to teach everyone that marriage is sacred.

The First Marriage

The first marriage took place in the garden of Eden when God joined Adam and Eve as husband and wife. This was not a sacrament. Remember, the sacraments were instituted by Christ many centuries later.

The Sacrament of Matrimony

In the catechism definition, notice the words "for life." When a man and woman have been joined in a lawful Christian marriage and have once lived together as husband and wife, no power on earth can break that bond. Death alone can end it. The words of the marriage ceremony show this: "Will you take each other, for better, for worse, for richer, for poorer, in sickness and in health, until death"? Each answers, "I will."

A priest must perform the ceremony and witness the marriage vows. Two other persons must act also as witnesses to the marriage.

The ideal Catholic wedding takes place at a Nuptial Mass. The wedding ceremony takes place first and is followed by the Nuptial Mass. This is a Mass especially for the bride and groom. They should receive Holy Communion at it. What greater gift could they receive on their wedding day than Christ Himself?

Why is Matrimony a sacrament? Because the love shared between the man and the woman is a sign of the love Christ shares with the Church. Love purifies and sanctifies the married couple. As we hear in Genesis, "It is not good for man to be alone." Because God loves little children so much that He wants them to be born and loved and well cared for in body, mind, and soul. He loves their parents so much and He rejoices in the bringing of children into the world. He puts a strong love into the hearts of the parents and gives them this sacrament which brings them the strength and grace to perform all the duties of a good Christian father and mother.

The Domestic Church

The domestic church is a term we use to describe what mothers and fathers create within their family. Domestic means "home." So even though there are limitations to what a family can do to turn their home into a church, they can still create a church-like atmosphere by praying together, hanging up sacred art on the walls, and reading Scripture together, among other things. The domestic church is a vital part of a child growing up to practice his faith later in life. What can you do to help your parents create a domestic church in your home?

The Catholic Home

To be a good father or mother is no easy task. It is the duty of the father to love, guide, protect, and care for his wife and children. He is the head of the family, as St. Joseph was of the Holy Family. The mother is to care for the home. She must cook, clean, sew, and do the hundred other jobs that a home demands. The mother and father must love one another, give good example to their children, and see to it that their little ones grow in the love and fear of God. "The family that prays together, stays together" is a slogan that every Catholic family should make its own.

We have been talking about the duties of a mother and father. Do the children have duties? We know they have. We learned about the love and respect that we owe our parents when we studied the fourth commandment. After studying about the sacrament of Matrimony, we realize better than ever how important is the place of the children in the family. Perhaps we appreciate a little better, too, the position held by our parents. They take the place of God, and they are responsible to Him for the children He has sent them. Let us pray daily for our mothers and fathers. Let us do all we can to make our homes like the home in Nazareth.

FOR ME TO STUDY

Catechism Lesson

1005. Q. What is the sacrament of matrimony?

A. The sacrament of matrimony is the sacrament which unites a Christian man and woman in lawful marriage.

- *Where did the first marriage take place?*
- *Tell some of the ways in which you can help make your home like the little home in Nazareth.*
- *Why is this slogan a good one for your home? "The family that prays together stays together"*
- *What is the best way for Catholics to be married?*

FOR ME TO REMEMBER

1. Matrimony is sacred, and only death can break the bonds that join a man and woman.
2. By obeying my father and mother, I show my love for them and for God.
3. I owe my parents great love, respect, and obedience.

FOR ME TO DO

1. Pray every day for my parents.
2. Thank God for this sacrament which gives special graces to my father and mother.
3. Try to do some good deed every day for Father and mother, to show them I care for them.
4. Do something special for their wedding anniversary.

Anointing of the Sick, Holy Orders, Matrimony

Write your answers on a separate sheet of paper

PART I *Matching*

Match each term given in Column I with its meaning in Column II:

Column I	Column II
A. Sacrament of the Living	1. A place of study for the priesthood
B. Seminary	2. Holy Communion received when one is in danger of death
C. Holy Orders	3. The sacrament uniting a man and a woman for life
D. Nuptial Mass	4. Last anointing
E. Consecrated Vocation	5. The Mass at which a special blessing is given the bride and groom
F. Matrimony	6. A sacrament to be received in the state of grace.
G. Sacramental Grace	7. The sacrament through which a man becomes a priest
H. Holy Viaticum	8. A call to serve God
I. Anointing of the Sick	9. The special grace which each sacrament gives

PART II *Completion*

Complete the following sentences by supplying the missing words:

1. We know from the Epistle of (1) that Christ gave us the sacrament of the Anointing of the Sick.
2. We pray to (2) for the grace of a happy death.
3. Anointing of the Sick gives (3) and (4) to the soul and sometimes to the (5).
4. In the sacrament of Holy Orders the priest receives the power

to offer the (6), to (7), and to administer the (8).

5. A priest is another (9), and for that reason should receive our greatest (10).
6. Holy Orders is a sacrament that is received only (11) because it leaves an (12) mark on the soul.
7. The greatest gift the newly married couple can receive on their wedding day is (13).
8. The model for the Catholic home is the (14) and a good slogan for that home is (15).
9. A Catholic marriage takes place in church in the presence of a priest and (16).

PART III *Yes or No*

Answer the following questions with Yes or No:

1. Was the sacrament of Matrimony instituted in the Garden of Eden?
2. May Anointing of the Sick be received only once?
3. May Matrimony be received only once?
4. May Holy Orders be received only once?
5. May an infant receive the sacrament of the Anointing of the Sick?
6. May an unconscious person receive the sacrament of the Anointing of the Sick?
7. Were the Apostles the first priests?
8. May a Catholic be married before a Justice of the Peace?
9. If a married man and woman do not get along, may they get a divorce and marry someone else?

NON ABE
BIS
LIENOS
NON ASS
VMES NO
MEN
TVI
S. CIPRIAN
S. CLEMENS

UNIT

5 The Sacramentals and Prayer

CHAPTER 26
Another Means of Grace

The twins, Emily and Susan, received beautiful crystal rosaries for their birthday. After they had them blessed, they prayed a rosary in church. Susan said the prayers devoutly and thought about each of the mysteries. Emily played with her beads and thought only about how pretty they were. Susan prayed her rosary well. Because she did, she received the actual grace God had for her. Emily did not pray the rosary properly so she did not receive the grace this sacramental could have given her.

LESSON 50
Sacramentals

A sacramental is a holy thing which should be used in a holy way. The help we receive from using a sacramental depends on how devoutly we use it. The catechism tells us that *sacramentals are holy things or actions of which the Church makes use to obtain for us from God spiritual and temporal favors.*

The sacramentals most used by Catholics are: holy water, blessed candles, ashes, palms, crucifixes, medals, rosaries, scapulars, and images of our Lord, the Blessed Virgin, and the saints.

The sign of the cross is another sacramental that is frequently used. The priest makes the Sign of the Cross often at holy Mass. When you go to confession the priest makes the Sign of the Cross when he forgives your sins. Holy water, candles, ashes, and other sacramentals receive the power to obtain for us from God spiritual and temporal favors when they are blessed with the Sign of

The Miraculous Medal is an example of a sacramental. Do you know the story of St. Catherine Laboré? If not, go look it up!

the Cross. Can you think of any times when you use this powerful sacramental? What other sacramentals do you use?

Using Sacramentals

How can water, a medal, or a piece of cloth help to save our souls? By themselves these things have no power to help or save us; but as sacramentals blessed by the Church, they do give spiritual help, when we use them correctly.

To use them correctly means to treat them with respect. For example: to keep blessed palms in a special place, to wear a medal with devotion, to care for crucifixes or statues and keep them in a place of honor, to use holy water with faith, and to pray the rosary well.

Are we obliged to use sacramentals? Must a Catholic wear a scapular, use holy water, or pray the rosary? No, the sacramentals are not necessary for salvation; but the prayers, pious objects, and sacred signs of the Church are aids to salvation.

Like the sacraments, the sacramentals help us to get grace; however, they are different from the sacraments in the following ways:

THE SACRAMENTS

1. were instituted by Christ;
2. are limited to seven;
3. give or increase sanctifying grace if received worthily.

THE SACRAMENTALS

1. were founded by the Church;
2. are many and varied according to the direction of the Church;
3. provide means to obtain actual grace if used with faith and reverence and thus, indirectly, gain sanctifying grace.

If we use the sacramentals with faith and devotion, they will obtain for us many blessings for body and soul. When the sacramentals are used properly they:

1. take away venial sin;
2. obtain graces for us;
3. remit temporal punishment;
4. protect us from evil spirits and temptations;
5. secure for us many blessings.

We should appreciate these extra helps to obtain grace and use them as God wishes us to do. We should be careful to use them with faith and not as objects of superstition. We must remember that they are useless of themselves. The prayer and the blessings of the Church give them their power.

O MARIE CONÇUE SANS PÉCHÉ PRIEZ POUR NOUS QUI AVONS RECOURS A VOUS

FOR ME TO STUDY

Catechism Lesson

1052. Q. What is a sacramental?

A. A sacramental is anything set apart or blessed by the Church to encourage good thoughts and to increase devotion, and through these movements of the heart to remit venial sin.

1053. Q. How do the sacramentals encourage good thoughts and increase devotion?

A. The sacramentals encourage good thoughts by recalling to our minds some special reason for doing good and avoiding evil; especially by reminding us of some holy person, event, or thing through which blessings have come to us. They increase devotion by fixing our minds on particular virtues and by helping us to understand and desire them.

1063. Q. Which is the chief sacramental used in the Church?

A. The chief sacramental used in the Church is the Sign of the Cross.

- *Other commonly used sacramentals include: holy water, candles, ashes, palms, crucifixes, rosaries, images of our Lord, of Mary, and the saints.*

FOR ME TO REMEMBER

1. The Church makes use of sacramentals to obtain spiritual and temporal favors from God for us.
2. Sacramentals do not have power in themselves, as the sacraments do. Their power comes from the prayer of the Church and from our own belief and devotion.

FOR ME TO DO

1. Get some holy water from church and use it every morning and night.
2. Wear a scapular or a scapular medal.
3. Learn about many sacramentals and use them.
4. Always carry a rosary and use it every day.

CHAPTER 27

Lifting Our Minds and Hearts to God

LESSON 51

Prayer

We are told that the Curé of Ars, a very holy priest, noticed a peasant who used to spend hours before the Blessed Sacrament. The saintly priest observed that the old man's lips never moved but his eyes remained fixed upon the tabernacle. One day the priest asked him what he said to our dear Lord during his long visits in Church. The poor man replied. "I look at Him and He looks at me." No words were necessary to express the love that filled the heart of this humble man for Jesus. *Prayer is the lifting up of our minds and hearts to God.*

If our mind is not on our prayer our thoughts will wander away. We then offend Him to whom we are speaking because we do not pay attention to what we are saying to Him. Christ says, "And I say to you, ask, and it shall be opened to you" (Lk. 11:9–10). At another time our Lord said, "Ask the Father anything in My name and He will give it to you" (Mt. 21:22). God will always hear our prayers if we pray properly. He may not give us exactly what we ask for, but He will give us what is best for us.

Christ Teaches Us to Pray

One day when our Lord was at prayer, the disciples came to Him and asked Him to teach them to pray. Immediately Christ turned and taught His disciples to pray the Our Father. That is the best prayer of all. It is a prayer to God and we ask from Him

the best things for ourselves and others and in the way in which they should be asked. *The Our Father is the best of all prayers because it is the Lord's Prayer, taught us by Jesus Christ Himself.*

Why We Pray

We pray: first, to adore God; second, to thank Him for His favors; third, to obtain from Him the pardon of our sins and the remission of their punishment; fourth, to ask graces and blessings for ourselves and others.

To adore God: Only God is deserving of adoration. Adoration means telling God in words and actions that He is supreme, that He is above everyone and everything. By adoration we recognize that He is our Creator and Father. Sometimes our adoration is shown by our words in prayer. At other times we adore God by actions such as: a reverent genuflection to Jesus in the Blessed Sacrament; a fervent sign of the cross; a bowing of the head at the sound of the Holy Name; a loving look toward the tabernacle when leaving the church. These and many other actions are examples of adoration even though no word is spoken.

To thank Him for His favors: Everyone likes to be thanked for favors, and God loves grateful hearts. Jesus lamented, when He had cleansed the ten lepers, that only one returned to give thanks. Were we to thank God for His many favors we would be praying to Him day and night. What are some of the benefits for which we should thank God? We should thank Him for our faith, the Mass, Holy Communion, for health, work, talents, success and pleasures, the food we eat, the water we drink, the air we breathe. We should thank Him for a lovely day or for a good mark at school. We should even thank Him for suffering, because God always wills it or permits it for our own good. It is well to remember that gratitude for past favors is the best means of obtaining new ones.

To obtain from Him pardon of our sins and the remission of their punishment: All of us have offended God in big or little ways. All of us need to beg His pardon for breaking His laws or for going against His wishes. How necessary it is for us to get into the habit of making an act of contrition after we have committed sin. We should often tell God how sorry we are for our sins because He is so good in Himself and always so good to us!

To ask graces and blessings for ourselves and others: God wants us to beg Him for the graces and blessings that are needed by ourselves and others. Our Lord also approved of group prayer when He said, "For where two or three are gathered together for My sake, there am I in the midst of them" (Mt. 18:20). Thus the prayers of a family praying together, or a group of people, or a congregation in church are very pleasing to God. It is a bond of our oneness in the Mystical Body of Christ. It is true God knows our needs better than we do, but He is more pleased when we beg Him for spiritual and temporal favors.

For Whom We Should Pray

We should pray especially for ourselves, for our parents, relatives, friends, and enemies, for sinners, for the souls in purgatory, for the pope, bishops, and priests of the Church, and for the officials of our country. Our prayer is certainly unselfish if we include the whole world in our prayers! Our prayers are always answered, but not always in the way we think they should be. Can you think of a reason why?

Why do we not always obtain what we pray for? *We do not always obtain what we pray for, either because we have not prayed properly or because God sees that what we are asking would not be good for us.*

How We Should Pray

It is not always necessary to use a prayer book or rosary when we pray. *We may use our own words in praying to God, and it is well to do so often.* We should get used to speaking to Him as we would do to our friends.

We usually begin and end our prayers with the sign of the cross. We make the sign of the cross to express two important mysteries of the Christian religion, the Blessed Trinity and the Incarnation.

Christ is our model in prayer, as in all other things. We are told many times that in His life "He spent the night in the prayer of God," or, "He went up into the mountain to pray." He has told us in one of His beautiful sermons to pray always. Let us pray especially every morning and night, in time of danger and temptation, and before and after meals. If we offer our work, play, joys, and sufferings to God they become prayers too. With Christ our perfect example, let us often turn our hearts to our Father in heaven.

Adoration, petition, intercession, and thanksgiving are the four types of prayer.

FOR ME TO STUDY

Catechism Lesson

1099. Q. What is prayer?

A. Prayer is the lifting up of our minds and hearts to God, to adore Him, to thank Him for His benefits, to ask His forgiveness, and to beg of Him all the graces we need whether for soul or body.

1124. Q. For what should we pray?

A. We should pray 1) For ourselves, for the blessings of soul and body that we may be devoted servants of God; 2) for the Church, for all spiritual and temporal wants, that the true Faith may be everywhere known and professed; 3) for our relatives, friends and benefactors, particularly for those we may in any way have injured; 4) for all men, for the protection of the good and conversion of the wicked, that virtue may flourish and vice disappear; 5) for our spiritual rulers, the Pope, our Bishops, priests and religious communities, that they may faithfully perform their sacred duties; 6) for our country and temporal rulers, that they may use their power for the good of their subjects and for the honor and glory of God.

1110. Q. Why does God not always grant our prayers?

A. God does not always grant our prayers for these and other reasons: 1) Because we may not pray in the proper manner; 2) that we may learn our dependence on Him, prove our confidence in Him, and merit rewards by our patience and perseverance in prayer. Prudent persons do not grant every request; why, then, should God do so?

1069. Q. How does the Sign of the Cross express the mystery of the Incarnation and death of our Lord?

A. The Sign of the Cross expresses the mystery of the Incarnation by reminding us that the Son of God, having become man, suffered death on the Cross.

3. Q. Why is the "Our Father" the most excellent of all prayers?

A. The "Our Father" is the most excellent of all prayers because our Lord Himself made it and because its petitions ask for all we can need for soul or body.

FOR ME TO REMEMBER

1. Prayer is thinking about God and talking to Him with loving attention.
2. We ought to pray often during the day, but especially in the morning and evening.
3. Jesus Christ taught us the Lord's Prayer, or the Our Father.
4. It is good to pray to God as we would speak with a friend, using our own words.

FOR ME TO DO

1. My list of "must" prayers will include each day: Morning Prayers, including Morning Offering; Night Prayers, including Act of Contrition; Angelus; Meal Prayers.
2. Make the sign of the cross slowly and with reverence.
3. Say often, "All for Thee, most Sacred Heart of Jesus."

Sacramentals and Prayers

Write your answers on a separate sheet of paper

PART I *Multiple Choice*

Choose the correct answer:

1. Sacramentals were instituted by:
   A. Christ.
   B. the Church.
   C. one of the saints.

2. Sacramentals take away:
   A. venial sin.
   B. original sin.
   C. mortal sin.

3. The best prayer is:
   A. Apostles' Creed.
   B. Our Father.
   C. Hail Mary.

4. Our greatest model for prayer is:
   A. St. Peter.
   B. our patron saint.
   C. Christ.

5. Sacramentals:
   A. provide means of grace.
   B. give sanctifying grace.
   C. give grace by themselves.

6. Prayer:
   A. must always be said aloud.
   B. is necessary for salvation.
   C. should be read from a book.

PART II *Matching*

Match each term in Column I with its meaning in Column II:

Column I	Column II
A. Sacramentals	1. The best prayer
B. Prayer	2. A prayer and a sacramental
C. Sign of the Cross	3. Highest form of prayer
D. Our Father	4. Important mystery of our religion
E. Blessed Trinity	5. Blessed objects
F. Holy Water	6. Gift of God
G. Adoration	7. Talking with God
H. Grace	8. A sacramental

PART III *Answer the following:*

1. Name four sacramentals that you use the most.
2. Tell the four reasons why we pray.
3. Name the two mysteries expressed by the sign of the cross.

Prayers

The Sign of the Cross

In the name of the Father, and of the Son, and of the Holy Spirit. Amen.

The Lord's Prayer

Our Father who art in heaven, hallowed be Thy name; Thy kingdom come; Thy will be done on earth as it is in heaven. Give us this day our daily bread; and forgive us our trespasses as we forgive those who trespass against us; and lead us not into temptation, but deliver us from evil. Amen.

The Hail Mary

Hail Mary, full of grace, the Lord is with thee; blessed art thou among women, and blessed is the fruit of thy womb, Jesus. Holy Mary, Mother of God, pray for us sinners, now and at the hour of our death. Amen.

Glory Be to the Father

Glory be to the Father, and to the Son, and to the Holy Spirit. As it was in the beginning, is now, and ever shall be, world without end. Amen.

The Apostles' Creed

I believe in God, the Father Almighty, Creator of heaven and earth; and in Jesus Christ, His only Son, Our Lord; who was conceived by the Holy Spirit, born of the Virgin Mary, suffered under Pontius Pilate, was crucified, died, and was buried. He descended into hell; the third day He arose again from the dead; He ascended into heaven, and sits at the right hand of God, the Father Almighty; from thence He shall come to judge the living and the dead. I believe in the Holy Spirit, the Holy Catholic Church, the communion of saints, the forgiveness of sins, the resurrection of the body, and life everlasting. Amen.

The Confiteor

Ordinary Form

I confess to almighty God
and to you, my brothers and sisters,
that I have greatly sinned
in my thoughts and in my words,
in what I have done,
and in what I have failed to do;
through my fault, through my fault,
through my most grievous fault;
therefore I ask blessed Mary ever-Virgin,
all the Angels and Saints,
and you, my brothers and sisters,
to pray for me to the Lord our God. Amen

Extraordinary Form

I confess to Almighty God,
to blessed Mary ever Virgin,
blessed Michael the Archangel,
blessed John the Baptist,
the holy Apostles Peter and Paul,
and to all the saints
that I have sinned exceedingly
in thought, word, and deed,
through my fault,
through my fault,
through my most grievous fault.
Therefore, I beseech blessed Mary ever Virgin,
blessed Michael the Archangel,
blessed John the Baptist,
the holy Apostles Peter and Paul,
and all the saints,
to pray for me to the Lord our God. Amen.

Morning Offering

O Jesus, through the Immaculate Heart of Mary, I offer Thee my prayers, works, joys and sufferings of this day for all the intentions of Thy Sacred Heart, in union with the Holy Sacrifice of the Mass throughout the world, in reparation for my sins, for the intentions of all our relatives and friends, and in particular for the intentions of the Hold Father. Amen.

The Angelus

V. The angel of the Lord declared unto Mary.
R. And she conceived of the Holy Spirit.

Hail Mary, full of grace! the Lord is with thee; blessed art thou among women, and blessed is the fruit of thy womb, Jesus. Holy Mary, Mother of God, pray for us sinners, now and at the hour of our death. Amen.

V. Behold the handmaid of the Lord.
R. Be it done unto me according to thy word.

Hail Mary, etc.

V. And the Word was made flesh.
R. And dwelt among us.

Hail Mary, etc.

V. Pray for us, O holy Mother of God.
R. That we may be made worthy of the promises of Christ.

Let Us Pray
Pour forth, we beseech Thee, O Lord, Thy grace into our hearts, that we to whom the Incarnation of Christ, Thy Son, was made known by the message of an angel, may by His passion and cross be brought to the glory of His resurrection, through the same Christ Our Lord. Amen.

Regina Coeli

(Said during Eastertide, Instead of the Angelus)

Queen of heaven, rejoice, Alleluia.
For He whom thou didst deserve to bear, Alleluia.
Hath risen as He said, Alleluia.
Pray for us to God, Alleluia.
V. Rejoice and be glad, O Virgin Mary! Alleluia.
R. Because Our Lord is truly risen, Alleluia.

Let Us Pray
O God, who by the resurrection of Thy Son, Our Lord Jesus Christ, have vouchsafed to make glad the whole world, grant, we beseech Thee, that, through the intercession of the Virgin Mary, His Mother, we may attain the joys of eternal life. Through the same Christ Our Lord. Amen.

Hail, Holy Queen

Hail, Holy Queen, Mother of Mercy; hail, our life, our sweetness, and our hope! To thee do we cry, poor banished children of Eve; to thee we do send up our sighs, mourning and weeping in this vale of tears. Turn, then, most gracious advocate, thine eyes of mercy toward us; and after this our exile, show unto us the blessed fruit of thy womb, Jesus. O clement, O loving, O sweet Virgin Mary!

An Act of Faith

O my God, I firmly believe that Thou art one God in three Divine Persons, Father, Son, and Holy Spirit; I believe that Thy Divine Son became man, and died for our sins, and that He will come to judge the living and the dead. I believe these and all the truths which the Holy Catholic Church teaches, because Thou hast revealed them, who canst neither deceive nor be deceived.

An Act of Hope

O my God, relying on Thy almighty power and infinite mercy and promises, I hope to obtain pardon of my sins, the help of Thy grace, and life everlasting, through the merits of Jesus Christ, my Lord and Redeemer.

An Act of Love

O my God, I love Thee above all things, with my whole heart and soul, because Thou art all-good and worthy of all love. I love my neighbor as myself for the love of Thee. I forgive all who have injured me, and ask pardon of all whom I have injured.

An Act of Contrition

O my God, I am heartily sorry for having offended Thee, and I detest all my sins, because of Thy just punishments, but most of all because they offend Thee, my God, who art all-good and deserving of all my love. I firmly resolve, with the help of Thy grace, to sin no more and to avoid the near occasions of sin.

The Blessing Before Meals

Bless us, O Lord, and these Thy gifts, which we are about to receive from Thy bounty, through Christ Our Lord. Amen.

Grace After Meals

We give Thee thanks for all Thy benefits, O Almighty God, who livest and reignest forever; and may the souls of the faithful departed, through the mercy of God, rest in peace. Amen.

The Mysteries of the Rosary

The Five Joyful Mysteries

1. The Annunciation
2. The Visitation
3. The Birth of Our Lord
4. The Presentation of Our Lord in the Temple
5. The Finding of Our Lord in the Temple

The Five Luminous Mysteries

1. The Baptism of Our Lord in the Jordan
2. The Wedding Feast at Cana
3. Our Lord's Proclamation of the Kingdom of God
4. The Transfiguration of Our Lord
5. The Institution of the Eucharist

The Five Sorrowful Mysteries

1. The Agony of Our Lord in the Garden
2. The Scourging at the Pillar
3. The Crowning With Thorns
4. The Carrying of the Cross
5. The Crucifixion and Death of Our Lord

The Five Glorious Mysteries

1. The Resurrection of Our Lord
2. The Ascension of Our Lord into Heaven
3. The Descent of the Holy Spirit Upon the Apostles
4. The Assumption of Our Blessed Mother into Heaven
5. The Coronation of Our Blessed Mother in Heaven

The Immaculate Conception with the Fifteen Mysteries of the Rosary

Answer Key

Chapter 1

Part I: Matching

A-3
B-4
C-5
D-6
E-2
F-1
G-9
H-8
I-7
J-10

Part II: Yes or No

1. Yes
2. No
3. Yes
4. Yes
5. Yes
6. No
7. Yes
8. Yes
9. No
10. Yes

Part III: Multiple Choice

1. B
2. C
3. A
4. C
5. A

6. B
7. C
8. B
9. B
10. B

Part IV: Matching

1-F

2-D

3-G

4-J

5-E

6-A

7-H

8-B

9-I

10-C

Part V: Completion

1. limbo
2. God
3. man
4. one
5. holy
6. catholic or universal
7. apostolic
8. wisdom
9. understanding
10. counsel
11. fortitude
12. knowledge
13. piety
14. fear of the Lord

Chapter 2

Part I: Matching

A-2
B-3
C-7
D-13
E-11
F-12
G-4
H-6
I-5
J-1
K-15
L-9
M-10
N-8
O-14

Part II: Multiple Choice

1. A
2. A
3. B
4. B
5. A
6. B
7. C
8. A
9. B
10. B

Chapters 3–9

Part I: Which commandments tell us to do the following?

1. 4
2. 8
3. 5
4. 7
5. 5-6
6. 4
7. 5
8. 6
9. 5
10. 10
11. 6-9
12. 7
13. 8
14. 5
15. 7

Part II: Completion

1. Holy Spirit
2. word
3. looks
4. actions
5. respect
6. love
7. God's
8. spiritual
9. bodily
10. dishonesty.
11. satisfied
12. thoughts
13. desires
14. repair
15. lies

Part III: Multiple Choice

1. C
2. A
3. C
4. B
5. B
6. A
7. B

Chapters 10–15

Part I: Which precept of the Church is kept in each of these cases?

1. 5
2. 4
3. 1
4. 5
5. 4
6. 1
7. 3
8. 2
9. 5

Part I: Matching

A-6
B-7
C-4
D-9
E-8
F-1
G-5
H-2
I-3

Chapters 16–19

Part I: Matching

1-C

2-H

3-A

4-F

5-E

6-G

7-B

8-D

Part II: Completion

1. Holy Communion
2. Penance and Reconciliation
3. Anointing of the Sick
4. Matrimony
5. sacrilege
6. Baptism
7. Confirmation
8. Holy Orders
9. original sin
10. the priest
11. dead
12. saint
13. Baptism
14. Sanctifying
15. pour water over the forehead while saying at the same time: "I baptize you in the name of the Father and of the Son and of the Holy Spirit
16. cleansed of original sin, given sanctifying grace, made a child of God and a member of His Church
17. unless a man be born again of water and the Holy Spirit he can not enter into the kingdom of God.

Part III: Yes or No

1. No
2. Yes
3. No
4. Yes
5. Yes
6. Yes
7. Yes
8. Yes
9. Yes
10. No

Part IV: Completion

1. Christians
2. soldiers
3. bishop
4. Last Supper
5. contained
6. offered
7. received
8. color
9. taste
10. weight
11. shape
12. bread
13. wine

Chapter 20

Part I: Yes or No

1. Yes
2. No
3. Yes
4. No
5. Yes
6. No
7. No
8. No
9. Yes
10. No

Part II: Multiple Choice

1. B
2. B
3. B
4. C
5. B
6. A
7. B
8. C
9. B
10. A

Part III: Ordinary or Proper

1. Ordinary
2. Proper
3. Ordinary
4. Ordinary
5. Proper
6. Ordinary
7. Proper
9. Ordinary

Part IV: Completion

1. sacrifice
2. Christ
3. bread
4. wine
5. priest
6. victim
7. consecration
8. faithful
9. Christ
10. Mass

Chapters 21–22

Part I: Matching

A-3
B-9
C-2
D-1
E-6
F-4
G-5
H-10
I-7
J-8

Part II: Yes or No

1. Yes
2. Yes
3. Yes
4. No
5. No
6. No
7. Yes
8. Yes
9. Yes

Part III: Multiple Choice

1. B
2. A
3. C
4. A
5. B
6. C
7. A
8. B
9. C
10. A

Part IV: Matching

1-D
2-F
3-G
4-I
5-H
6-B
7-D
8-A
9-E

Chapters 23–25

Part I: Matching

A-6
B-1
C-7
D-5
E-8
F-3
G-9
H-2
I-4

Part II: Completion

1. St. James
2. St. Joseph
3. health
4. strength
5. body
6. Mass
7. teach
8. sacraments
9. Christ
10. respect
11. once
12. indelible
13. Christ in Holy Communion
14. Holy Family
15. the family that prays together, stays together
16. two witnesses

Part III: Yes or No

1. No
2. No
3. No
4. Yes
5. Yes
6. Yes
7. Yes
8. No
9. No

Chapters 26–27

Part I: Multiple Choice

1. B
2. A
3. B
4. C
5. A
6. B

Part II: Matching

A-5
B-7
C-2
D-1
E-4
F-8
G-3
H-6

Part III: Answer the following

1. holy water; candles; ashes; palms; crucifixes; medals; etc.
2. to adore God; to thank God; to obtain pardon for sin; to ask for graces and blessings
3. the Unity of God; the Trinity; the Redemption

Image Credits

front cover Light of the World, c.1851-53 (oil on canvas), Hunt, William Holman (1827-1910) / English, By Kind Permission of the Warden, Fellows, and Scholars of Keble College, Oxford / Bridgeman Images

pvii-1 The Resurrection, 15th century (tempera on panel), Master of the Osservanza, (fl.c.1436) / Italian, Founders Society Purchase / Gift of Mr & Mrs Henry Ford II / Bridgeman Images

p 2–3, 58–59, 74–75, 88–89, 100–101, 106–107, 114–115, 120–121, 124–125, 134–135, 138–139, 146–147, 152–153, 158–159, 162–163, 170–171, 182–183, 188–189, 196–197, 204–205, 238–239, 262–263, 272–273, 278–279, 284–285, 292–293, 298–299 Christ and Saint John the Baptist in Hagia Sophia (mosaic), Tarker / Bridgeman Images

p3 Reaching hands from The Creation of Adam of Michelangelo illustration reproduction by Freeda Michaux/Shutterstock

p6 The Creation of the World (oil on canvas), Le Sueur, Eustache (1617-55) / French, Bridgeman Images

p7 Eternal Now, Philip Steury Photography/Shutterstock

p9 Shield of the Trinity by TAN Books

p11 White Angel or Myrrhbearers on Christ's Grave, photo by PavleMarjanovic/ Shutterstock

p12 Archangel Michael Sculpture, photo by aSuruwataRi/Shutterstock

p15 Guardian angel protecting children near a cliff, early 1900s illustration, by Victorian Traditions/Shutterstock

p16 Eve giving Adam the forbidden fruit (photo), Godong / Bridgeman Images

p17 The Immaculate Conception (oil on canvas), Giovanni Battista Tiepolo, public domain via Wikimedia Commons

p18–19 Earthly Paradise (oil on panel), Brueghel, Jan the Younger (1601-78) / Flemish, Bridgeman Images

p21 Marble statue of the Virgin Mary, photo by Kamira/Shutterstock

p22 Red apple with missing bite, photo by Weerachai Khamfu/Shutterstock

p25 Victorian greeting card of an angel and two children praying, c. 1880 (colour litho), English School, (19th century) / English, Photo © David Pearson / Bridgeman Images

p26 The Madonna delle Ombre, 1450 (fresco), Angelico, Fra (Guido di Pietro) (c.1387-1455) / Italian, Photo © Raffaello Bencini / Bridgeman Images

p26 Adoration of the Magi, 1857 (oil on card), Flandrin, Hippolyte (1809-64) / French, Bridgeman Images

p28 Holy card, dedicated to the Sacred Heart, 1906 (printed card), French School, (19th century) / French, Bridgeman Images

p29 Jesus Teaching (gouache on paper), © Look and Learn / Bridgeman Images

p30 The Descent into Limbo, 1442 (fresco), Angelico, Fra (Guido di Pietro) (c.1387 1455) / Italian, Photo © Nicolò Orsi Battaglini / Bridgeman Images
p33 A free flying white dove by Elzza/Shutterstock
p35 Golden monstrance by MARI TERE/Shutterstock
p36 A free flying white dove by Elzza/Shutterstock
p36 Mary receiving the gifts of the Holy Spirit, detail (tempera on wood), Master of Lluca (13th century) / Spanish, © Iberfoto / Bridgeman Images
p37 Faith, Hope, and Love (chromolitho), European School, (19th century), Look and Learn / Valerie Jackson Harris Collection / Bridgeman Images
p39 Our Lady of Fatima, Chambers, Restored Traditions
p40 Saint Peter with key near St. Peter's Basilica, photo by Mykola Ivashchenko/ Shutterstock
p42–43 Giving of the Keys to St. Peter, from the Sistine Chapel, 1481 (fresco), Perugino, Pietro (c.1445-1523) / Italian, Bridgeman Images
p44 Bishop goes to Mass by wideonet/Shutterstock
p44–45 St. Peter's Square by Marti Bug Catcher/Shutterstock
p47 The Forerunners of Christ with Saints and Martyrs, 1423-24 (egg tempera on wood), Angelico, Fra (Guido di Pietro) (c.1387-1455) / Italian, Bridgeman Images
p48 The Church Militant and Triumphant, 1365-1367 (fresco), Andrea di Bonaiuto (Andrea da Firenze) (fl.1343-77) / Italian, Bridgeman Images
p50 Girl praying the Rosary by Africa Studio/Shutterstock
p53 The Assumption of the Virgin, c.1656 (oil on canvas), Champaigne, Philippe de (1602-74) / French, Bridgeman Images
p59 Moses and the Ten Commandments, Uptton, Clive (1911-2006) / English, © Look and Learn / Bridgeman Image
p60 Elderly woman sitting in wheelchair talking to her granddaughter, by Mallika Home Studio/Shutterstock
p62 Golden crucifix by gdvcom/Shutterstock
p63 Picture of the Immaculate Heart of Virgin Mary printed on a round wooden board. Taken in Bogota, Colombia by Felipe Mahecha/Shutterstock
p68 Mass in the Catholic Church by Cavee/Shutterstock
p 72–73 The Good Samaritan, c.1530s (tempera on wood), Campagnola, Domenico (fl.1517-62) / Italian, Gift of the Samuel H. Kress Foundation / Bridgeman Images
p75 The Finding of the Saviour in the Temple (oil on canvas), William Holman Hunt (1827–1910), public domain via Wikimedia Commons
p77 The Holy Family, Nazareth, Israel, Godong / Bridgeman Images
p79 Blue pen by Dmitriy Kazitsyn/Shutterstock
p80 Jesus Prays in the garden Gethsemane by Freedom Studio/Shutterstock
p82 Little girl with laundry by Pixel-Shot/Shutterstock
p83 S Bernardus Abbas Claravallis (colour litho), French School, (19th century) /

French, © Look and Learn / Bridgeman Images
p84 The death of Absalom, Hole, William Brassey (1846-1917) / English, © Look and Learn / Bridgeman Images
p86 Boy with a helmet and a blue backpack riding a bike by Ljupco Smokovski/ Shutterstock
p89 Priest celebrates Mass at the church by wideonet/Shutterstock
p91 The Good Samaritan (gouache on paper), © Look and Learn / Bridgeman Images
p92 The death of Abel (coloured engraving), German School, (19th century) / German, © Look and Learn / Bridgeman Images
p95 Christ driving the Traders from the Temple (oil on canvas), El Greco (1541–1614), public domain via Wikimedia Commons
p97 Baseball glove by StefanoT/Shutterstock
p98 St Francis preaching to the Birds (engraving), English School, (19th century) / English, © Look and Learn / Bridgeman Images
p101 Stained glass window depicting Maria Goretti, photo by Reinhard Müller, public domain via Wikimedia Commons
p102 Gala apples in rattan bowl by PIXbank CZ/Shutterstock
p105 Virgin Mary, digital illustration by Andrea Danti/Shutterstock
p107 Hand taking book from the shelf by donatas1205/Shutterstock
p108 Pink bike by PERLA BERANT WILDER/Shutterstock
p115 Marble statue of Jesus Christ by Kamira/Shutterstock
p117 Saint Athanasius Icon, Bridgeman Images
p121 Jesus falls while carrying the cross, Le Sueur, Eustache (1617-55) / French, Luisa Ricciarini / Bridgeman Images
p122 Thomas Aquinas, Ros, P. (19th century) / Spanish, © Look and Learn / Bridgeman Images
p122 Girl sitting on floor and reading book by Syda Productions/Shutterstock
p127 High Five line after a children's baseball game by Suzanne Tucker/Shutter-stock
p131 Moses Receives the Tablets of the Law from God on Mount Sinai (colour litho), French School, (19th century) / French, © Archives Charmet / Bridge-man Images
p132–133 Triumph of Catholic Doctrine, Andrea di Bonaiuto (Andrea da Firenze) (fl.1343-77) / Italian, Bridgeman Images
p140 Saint-Jacques church. Sunday morning catholic mass. Priest. Celebration of the Eucharist. Sallanches. France, Godong / Bridgeman Images
p142 Sunday Missal booklet by Lester Balajadia / Shutterstock
p145 Hymns for Christmas Mass, Villemomble, France, Godong / Bridgeman Images
p147 Woman confessing by ravipat/Shutterstock
p148 Children going to First Holy Communion by wideonet/Shutterstock

p151 Annunciation, Hole, William Brassey (1846-1917) / English, © Look and Learn / Bridgeman Images
p153 Forty days in the wilderness, tempted by Satan, Hole, William Brassey (1846-1917) / English, © Look and Learn / Bridgeman Images
p154 Candy jar by Billion Photos/Shutterstock
p157 Cross made of ashes by Thoom/Shutterstock
p159 Catholic priest collects money for the church by Martin Podzorny / Shutterstock
p160 The widow's mite (gouache on paper), Uptton, Clive (1911-2006) / English, © Look and Learn / Bridgeman Images
p163 Gold wedding rings by Luca Santilli/Shutterstock
p165 Catholic wedding by MNStudio/Shutterstock
p168–169 Interior of Antwerp cathedral with the Seven Sacraments, 1590 (oil on canvas), Steenwyck, Hendrik van (1550-1603) / Flemish, Bridgeman Images
p170 Rose bush by Kisialiou Yury/Shutterstock
p172 The Last Supper (oil on panel), Macip, Vicente Juan (Juan de Juanes) (c.1510-79) / Spanish, Bridgeman Images
p177 The Seven Sacraments, English School, (19th century) / English, © Look and Learn / Bridgeman Images
p181 The Seven Sacraments (colour litho), French School, (20th century) / French, Bridgeman Images
p185 Baptism by mylu/Shutterstock
p190–191 Pentecost, 1732 (oil on canvas),
p193 Priest with parents and children before the First Holy Communion by wideonet/Shutterstock
p195 Communion at the Church of the Trinity, 1877 (oil on canvas), Gervex, Henri (1852-1929) / French, Bridgeman Images
p197 Bowl of Communion Wafers by stockcreations/Shutterstock
p206 Mass in the Catholic Church by Cavee/Shutterstock
p207 Christ carrying the Cross (chromolitho), European School, (19th century) / European, Look and Learn / Valerie Jackson Harris Collection / Bridgeman Images
p210–211 Grapevine by Miiisha/Shutterstock
p217 Christ Blessing, c.1520 (oil on wood), Solario, Andrea (c.1466-1524) / Italian, Bridgeman Images
p218 Saint Anthony of Padua (colour litho), Italian School, (20th century) / Italian, © Look and Learn / Bridgeman Images
p221 Pair of cruets, Catholic Mass, Dalat, Vietnam, Godong / Bridgeman Images
p224 The Visitation Monastery, Francis de Sales (1567-1622), Marclaz, France, (photo), Godong / Bridgeman Images
p228 The Lord's Prayer (colour litho), English School, (19th century) / English, Look and Learn / Valerie Jackson Harris Collection / Bridgeman Images

p230 Hands of Catholic priest on altar with Crucifix by Calamity Jane/Shutterstock
p237 The Adoration of the Mystic Lamb, from the Ghent Altarpiece, detail of lower half of central panel, 1432 (oil on panel), © Lukas - Art in Flanders VZW / Purchased with the Director's Discretionary Fund, 1970 / Bridgeman Images
p239 The Institution of the Confession (colour litho), Angelico, Fra (c.1387-1455) (after) / Italian, © Look and Learn / Bridgeman Images
p243 Contrition erases sin, a man hides in Jesus' arms to obtain forgiveness, Unknown Artist, (20th century), Luisa Ricciarini / Bridgeman Images
p250 Valle Romita Polyptych: detail of st Thomas Aquinas (tempera on panel, ca. 1400), Fabriano, Gentile da (c.1370-1427) / Italian, Luisa Ricciarini / Bridgeman Images
p253 The Confession (wood), Domenico di Niccolo dei Cori (c.1375-1450) / Italian, Bridgeman Images
p255 The Confession (oil on canvas), Longhi, Pietro (c.1701-85) / Italian, Cameraphoto Arte Venezia / Bridgeman Images
p257 Old wooden confessional by Jaroslaw Grudzinski/Shutterstock
p258 The Ten Lepers, Uptton, Clive (1911-2006) / English, © Look and Learn / Bridgeman Images
p262 A baseball and wooden bat by Mike Flippo/Shutterstock
p273 Extreme Unction, c.1637-40 (oil on canvas), Poussin, Nicolas (1594-1665) / French, Bridgeman Images
p279 I have called thee by thy name (chromolitho), French School, (19th century) / French, © Look and Learn / Bridgeman Images
p286 The Holy Family, English School, (19th century) / English, © Look and Learn / Bridgeman Images
p290–291 The Forerunners of Christ with Saints and Martyrs, 1423-24 (egg tempera on wood), Angelico, Fra (Guido di Pietro) (c.1387-1455) / Italian, Bridgeman Images
p293 Christian medals, Saint-Gervais, France, Godong / Bridgeman Images
p295 Apparition of the Virgin to St. Catherine Laboure (1806-76) 31st July 1830, 1835 (oil on canvas), Le Cerf, (fl.1835) / French, © Archives Charmet / Bridgeman Images
p297 Bottle of holy water by pedrolieb/Shutterstock
p301 The boy Samuel praying, Lawson, John (19th century) / English, © Look and Learn / Bridgeman Images
p314 Interior of a Scriptorium, School of Segovia (oil on panel), Spanish School, (16th century) / Spanish, Bridgeman Images